The Herbalism & Medicinal Remedies Book

A Complete Home Apothecary Guide to Herbal Medicine, Healing Herbs, and 200+ Time-Tested Plant-Based Recipes for Natural and Holistic Wellness

(Master Herbalist Handbook, Vol. 1)

By

Maeven Alder

Disclaimer

This publication is designed to provide reliable information on the subject matter only for educational purposes, and it is not intended to provide medical advice for any medical treatment. You should always consult your doctor or physician for guidance before you stop, start, or alter any prescription medications or attempt to implement the methods discussed. This book is published independently by the author and has no affiliation with any brands or products mentioned within it. The author hereby disclaims any responsibility or liability whatsoever that is incurred from the use or application of the contents of this publication by the purchaser or reader. The purchaser or reader is hereby responsible for his or her own actions.

Other Books By Maeven Alder

Advanced Herbalism & Medicinal Remedies Book (Master Herbalist Handbook, Vol. 2)

Table of Contents

About the Author

Maeven Alder is a plant-hearted herbalist, writer, and teacher who believes healing begins with remembering. Her path into herbalism unfolded quietly—through tending gardens, making tea by moonlight, and learning to listen to what the plants were saying.

Rooted in folk tradition and shaped by lived experience, Maeven's approach to plant medicine is gentle, intuitive, and deeply personal. She teaches and writes for people who are just beginning their herbal journey—those who want to slow down, take care of themselves, and reconnect with the earth beneath their feet.

Maeven believes you don't need to be an expert to start using herbs. You just need a little curiosity, a few good plants, and the courage to trust your own senses. Her work centers around helping people become their own healers—one remedy, one cup of tea, one season at a time.

Through workshops, gatherings, and now this book, her mission is simple: to help others find their way back to the plants that have always been waiting.

Introduction – Welcome to Your Herbal Path

"You don't have to live off-grid to live closer to nature. Sometimes, it starts with a single leaf in a cup."

Welcome. Truly.

If this is your first time exploring herbalism, I'm honored to walk with you. If you've already dipped your toes into this green path—maybe sipping chamomile tea to relax or applying aloe to a sunburn—then welcome back. No matter where you are in your journey, this book was written for you.

Whether you're seeking healing, self-reliance, connection, or simply a deeper relationship with nature, the world of herbs has something waiting for you. Not just in facts and formulas, but in stories, wisdom, and personal discovery.

This is not just a book. It's a doorway. A path. A return.

Why Herbalism? Why Now?

In a time when life moves fast and stress is constant, more and more people are looking for something real, something rooted. They want health, not just medicine. Balance, not just treatment. And that's where herbs come in.

Herbalism gives us tools to care for ourselves and our families in a way that is natural, empowering, and meaningful. It reminds us that healing doesn't always have to come from a pharmacy. Sometimes, it comes from your kitchen cabinet, garden bed, or windowsill.

Here's what draws so many people to herbs today:

- **They're accessible** – You don't need a degree to start learning. Anyone can begin.
- **They're empowering** – Herbs help you take control of your health and care.
- **They're gentle** – When used properly, most herbs support the body without harsh side effects.
- **They reconnect us** – To the land, to our ancestors, and to ourselves.

Herbalism is not just about fixing what's broken. It's about nourishing what's whole. And that's something we all need.

What This Book Is (and Isn't)

This book was not written to overwhelm you. It's not filled with hard-to-find herbs or complex recipes meant for professionals. Instead, it's an invitation—a warm, open door into the world of plants.

You won't need a fancy lab or a lifetime of training to use what's here. You'll find guidance for creating teas, tinctures, salves, and simple remedies using herbs that are easy to find and understand. You'll learn how to grow and harvest them, how to choose the right one for the moment, and how to build your own herbal toolkit over time.

What this book *is*:

- A companion for beginners and lifelong learners alike
- A practical guide rooted in safety and simplicity
- A blend of science, tradition, and intuition
- A bridge between modern life and ancient wisdom

What this book *isn't*:

- A quick-fix cure-all
- A replacement for emergency care or professional advice
- A rigid doctrine or dogma

Herbalism isn't about rules—it's about relationship. You won't just memorize herbs here. You'll *meet* them.

What You'll Learn Inside

This book is divided into three parts:

Part I: Roots & Wisdom

This is your foundation. You'll learn how herbs work in the body, what makes them effective, and how to begin recognizing the patterns behind the plants. We'll explore the four major herbal families, the basic language of herbal actions (like "cooling" or "astringent"), and the ethics of using herbs wisely.

Part II: The Working Apothecary

Now we get hands-on. You'll learn how to stock your herbal shelf, what tools you need (spoiler: not many), and which 40 herbs are most helpful to keep on hand. We'll explore how to grow your own healing garden—even in a small space—and how to harvest and store herbs the right way.

Part III: Crafting Remedies

Time to make magic. You'll dive into herbal teas, syrups, tinctures, salves, and kitchen recipes. You'll discover how to make medicines that taste good, work well, and support your body through every season. You'll also learn how to create your own formulas and design remedies with confidence and care.

By the end, you'll have a strong foundation and the freedom to explore, experiment, and grow.

Who This Book Is For

This book is for the everyday person—the busy parent, the tired teacher, the curious soul, the backyard gardener, the kitchen witch, the wellness seeker. You don't need to be a scientist or a shaman. If you've ever looked at a plant and wondered, *What could you teach me?*, then you are in the right place.

It's also for those who want to:

- Take more responsibility for their health
- Use natural approaches alongside modern medicine
- Connect with their ancestry or cultural roots
- Feel more in control, calm, and connected

And it's especially for those who are tired of feeling disconnected from their bodies and the natural world. You belong here.

A Personal Note…

I didn't grow up using herbs. Like many people, I was taught to trust doctors and prescriptions—and there's nothing wrong with that. But somewhere along the way, I started to feel like I had no say in my own wellness. I was reacting to health, not building it.

When I discovered herbalism, something changed. I started listening—to plants, to my body, to my needs. I found healing not just in what herbs *do*, but in how they make you *feel seen*. They meet you where you are and remind you that your body knows what it's doing. Sometimes it just needs a nudge.

That's why I wrote this book. Not to impress you, but to *empower* you. Because you don't have to become a master herbalist to be your own healer. You just need a little curiosity, a few good plants, and the willingness to learn.

How to Use This Book

You can read it cover to cover, or jump to the section that calls to you. Keep a notebook handy for reflections, recipes, or ideas. Try things. Taste things. Trust your senses.

Some chapters are educational. Others are practical. All are written with love and the hope that you'll not just learn—but *connect*.

A few reminders as you begin:

- Start small. One herb at a time.
- Work with herbs, not against your body.
- Safety first. Always cross-check when in doubt.
- Enjoy the process. Herbalism is slow, but full of joy.

One Final Welcome

You are now part of a long, beautiful lineage—of midwives, monks, gardeners, grandmothers, and green witches. People who believed that healing was more than just a pill—it was a relationship.

Whether you're here to soothe anxiety, build immunity, or simply reconnect with the earth, you're in the right place. The plants have always been here. Now it's your turn to meet them.

Take your time. Open your senses. Let this book be your guide, but let the plants be your teachers.

Let's begin.

PART I: ROOTS & WISDOM

Chapter 1

Ancient Plants, Modern Purpose

"Before there were pills, there were plants."

Herbalism—the practice of using plants for healing—is one of the oldest forms of medicine in the world. Long before modern hospitals and pharmacies, people turned to the earth for remedies. They used the leaves, roots, flowers, and seeds of plants to treat illness, boost energy, calm the mind, and nourish the body. And they still do.

In every corner of the world, people have relied on herbs. In Egypt, healers wrote herbal formulas on papyrus scrolls. In China, ancient books describe the effects of hundreds of herbs. Native peoples in North and South America passed down their knowledge through stories, ceremony, and hands-on teaching. In Europe, monks and midwives tended herbal gardens and recorded their observations in thick leather-bound books.

Though these traditions are old, they are far from outdated. Today, more and more people are turning back to herbal medicine—not because they reject science, but because they want to reconnect with something deeper and more natural.

What Is Herbalism, Really?

Herbalism is more than just making tea when you're sick. It's a way of working with plants to support health and healing. That might mean sipping chamomile before bed, rubbing lavender oil on your temples when you're stressed, or brewing ginger tea when you feel a cold coming on.

But it's also about connection—understanding the plants, how they grow, what they offer, and what they need. Herbalism invites us to slow down, observe, and listen.

You don't need to be a professional to practice herbalism. You just need curiosity, patience, and respect for the living world.

Why Herbs Still Matter Today

With all the modern medicines available, why do people still turn to herbs? Simple. Because they work—and often gently.

Here's why herbalism still matters:

- **Herbs are accessible.** You can grow many of them in your backyard or on a windowsill.
- **They're safe when used correctly.** Most herbs have been used for centuries with few side effects.
- **They support the whole body.** Herbs don't just target one symptom—they help bring balance to multiple systems.
- **They empower you.** You become more in tune with your health, your environment, and your choices.

In a world full of quick fixes, herbalism offers a slower, more thoughtful approach to wellness.

The Herbalist's Perspective

To be a herbalist isn't about memorizing hundreds of plants. It's about building relationships. It means noticing how a plant smells, how it feels in your hand, where it grows, and how your body responds when you use it.

Herbalists ask questions like:

- What does this plant want to teach me?
- How does it help the body heal itself?
- When should it be harvested?
- What kind of people or conditions benefit from this herb?

This way of thinking turns herbalism into more than just medicine—it becomes a way of life.

A Living Tradition

Modern herbalism blends old wisdom with new research. We now understand not just that herbs work, but often *why* they work—thanks to science. Still, the heart of herbalism remains rooted in nature and tradition.

Some people forage herbs from the wild. Others grow their own healing gardens. Many buy high-quality herbs from trusted herbal stores. However you begin, you're stepping into a practice that stretches back thousands of years—and still has so much to offer today.

Final Thoughts...

Herbalism is about remembering. It reminds us that we are part of nature, not separate from it. That health is a relationship, not just a result. And that healing doesn't always come in a bottle—it can come in a leaf, a cup of tea, or a quiet moment spent with a plant.

As we move forward into this book, you'll learn how herbs work, how to meet them, grow them, prepare them, and use them safely. But for now, just take this with you:

The plants have always been here. And they are ready to help.
All you have to do is begin.

Chapter 2

Inside the Leaf: How Herbs Work in the Body

"Herbs don't force healing. They help your body remember how to heal itself."

Before you start picking herbs, growing them, or making teas and tinctures, it's helpful to know how they actually work *inside* your body. Herbs may seem like simple plants, but they're filled with natural chemicals that gently support your body's own healing systems.

In this chapter, we'll break down how herbs work, what they do in your body, and how they feel when you take them. This isn't science just for experts—this is knowledge for *you*, the everyday herbalist.

Medicinal Compounds in Plants

Every herb contains its own mix of natural ingredients, called **plant compounds**. These are like tiny tools that help your body feel better, heal faster, and stay in balance.

Here are some of the most common ones:

- **Alkaloids** – Very powerful ingredients that affect the brain and nerves. (Example: caffeine in coffee or tea)
- **Flavonoids** – Help protect your cells and reduce swelling or pain.
- **Tannins** – Help tighten tissues (great for cuts or sore throats).
- **Mucilage** – Feels slimy and coats sore or dry places (like the throat or stomach).
- **Saponins** – Help clear out mucus and support the immune system.
- **Essential Oils** – Give the plant its smell and help fight germs. (Found in mint, lavender, thyme)

These compounds interact with human biology in complex ways—often working in synergy rather than isolation. Some of these work better in **water** (like teas), others in **alcohol** (like tinctures), and some in **oils** (like salves and rubs).

N.B: Herbs rarely do just one thing. A single plant may calm the nerves, support digestion, and reduce inflammation all at once. This multifaceted behavior is what makes plant medicine so profound—and so holistic.

What Herbs Do: Their Jobs in Your Body

Herbs don't just sit in your body—they do things. Herbalists give names to these actions, like "relaxing," "cleansing," or "boosting." These are called **herbal actions**.

Here are a few:

- **Adaptogens** – Help your body handle stress better. (Ashwagandha, tulsi)
- **Nervines** – Calm the nerves or help you sleep. (Chamomile, lemon balm)
- **Carminatives** – Ease gas, bloating, and stomach cramps. (Fennel, peppermint)
- **Astringents** – Help stop diarrhea or bleeding by tightening tissues. (Yarrow, raspberry leaf)
- **Demulcents** – Soften and soothe dry or sore places. (Marshmallow root)
- **Diuretics** – Help your body release extra water and flush out toxins. (Dandelion leaf)
- **Expectorants** – Help clear mucus from the lungs. (Mullein, thyme)

Think of it this way: herbs are like helpful friends, each with a role. Some calm you, some clean you out, some protect you. When you know what they *do*, you can choose the right one for what your body needs.

How Herbs Feel: Warm, Cool, Dry or Moist

In old healing traditions (like Ayurveda and Western herbalism), people noticed how herbs *feel* in the body. This isn't about flavor—it's about temperature, moisture, and energy.

This is called **herbal energetics**.

- **Warming herbs**: Make you feel warm, boost energy, and improve digestion. (Example: ginger, cinnamon)
- **Cooling herbs**: Calm heat, redness, or tension in the body. (Example: peppermint, violet)
- **Drying herbs**: Help reduce extra mucus or wetness. (Example: sage, green tea)
- **Moistening herbs**: Help when you're too dry—inside or out. (Example: licorice, marshmallow)

Matching energetics to a person's constitution—hot, cold, dry, or damp—helps prevent aggravation and creates more balanced outcomes. For example, if you have a dry cough, you want a moistening herb. If you have cold hands and slow digestion, you might need a warming one. Matching the *right herb to the right condition* is key.

How Herbs Help Your Body's Systems

Herbs don't work on just one part of your body. They support whole **body systems**—like your lungs, heart, stomach, and nerves.

Here's a simple breakdown:

Nervous System (Brain & Nerves)

- **Chamomile** and **valerian** help you relax and sleep.
- **Lemon balm** calms anxiety and lifts your mood.

Digestive System

- **Dandelion root** helps your stomach make more digestive juices.
- **Fennel** and **peppermint** reduce gas and cramping.

Immune System

- **Echinacea** boosts your body's defenses.
- **Elderberry** helps fight colds and viruses.

Respiratory System (Lungs)

- **Mullein** helps loosen mucus and soothe your lungs.
- **Thyme** fights bacteria and clears congestion.

Circulatory System (Heart & Blood)

- **Hawthorn** supports heart health and blood pressure.
- **Cayenne** improves blood flow and warms the body.

Urinary System (Bladder & Kidneys)

- **Cornsilk** and **dandelion leaf** help you pee more and clean your kidneys.

Reproductive System

- **Raspberry leaf** supports menstrual health.
- **Black cohosh** helps balance hormones during menopause.

Each herb has its favorite place in the body. Some are like cheerleaders for your nerves; others are like plumbers for your digestion. They all support balance in their own way.

Safety Tips: Using Herbs the Smart Way

Even though herbs are natural, they are still *medicine*. You must use them with care and respect.

Keep These Rules in Mind:

1. **Start Small** – Try a small dose first and see how your body reacts.
2. **Not for Everyone** – Some herbs are not safe in pregnancy or while breastfeeding. (Example: don't use strong herbs like mugwort or wormwood without advice.)
3. **Watch for Allergies** – If you're allergic to ragweed, avoid chamomile and echinacea.
4. **Mixing with Meds? Be Careful** – Herbs like **St. John's Wort** can interfere with medications like birth control or antidepressants.
5. **Not All Herbs Are Kid-Friendly** – Always lower the dose for children and avoid hot or bitter herbs unless guided.

Always check with a trusted herbalist or health provider before using strong herbs or mixing them with prescriptions.

Final Thoughts...

Herbs aren't just stuff you buy in a bottle. They are living allies. When you understand how they work *inside* you—what they do, how they feel, and where they act—you begin to build a relationship with them.

This chapter gave you the basics. Now you know:

- What's inside an herb (its chemistry)
- What it does in your body (its actions)
- How it feels in your body (its energetics)
- Where it works in your body (its system focus)
- And how to use it safely

With this knowledge, you can choose herbs that match what you *really need*—not just what's popular or trendy. You're learning to speak the language of the plants.

In the next chapter, we'll move from the body *back to the earth*. You'll learn how to meet your plant allies face-to-face—how to identify them, grow them, and gather them with care.

Your journey is just beginning. And the plants are waiting.

Chapter 3

Meeting Your Plant Allies

"The herbal path doesn't begin with a recipe. It begins with a relationship."

Herbalism is not just about remedies—it is about connection. The first time you sip a lemon balm infusion and feel your shoulders soften… the moment you catch the sweet, earthy scent of calendula petals… these are more than encounters. They're introductions. To walk the herbal path is to meet plants not merely as ingredients but as allies, companions, and teachers.

In this chapter, we go beyond theory. We start to cultivate a practical and spiritual relationship with our green companions. From recognizing their traits and growing them in your home apothecary garden to sourcing them ethically from the earth—they each have lessons to teach, energies to offer, and healing to share.

Understanding Herbal Families — Mint, Daisy, Carrot & Mallow

In the same way humans belong to family trees, plants belong to botanical families. These families are like groups of siblings with shared genetic traits, chemical compounds, and healing tendencies. Learning plant families helps herbalists identify new plants, predict their uses, and even avoid allergens or toxic relatives. Let's explore four foundational families in Western herbalism.

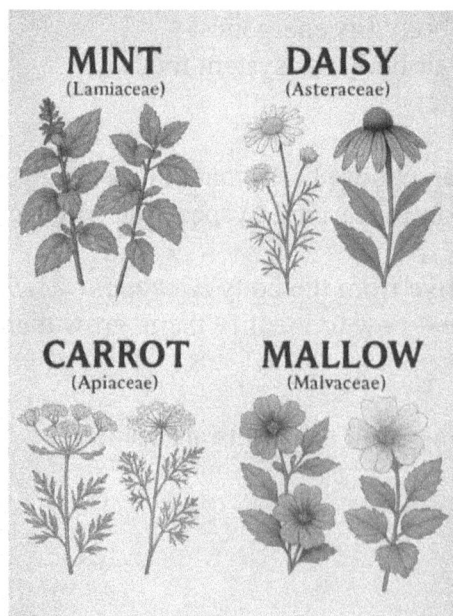

MINT (Lamiaceae) · DAISY (Asteraceae) · CARROT (Apiaceae) · MALLOW (Malvaceae)

Lamiaceae — The Mint Family

The mint family (Lamiaceae) is perhaps the most welcoming for new herbalists. These plants are easy to grow, widely available, and incredibly aromatic. Their volatile oils—responsible for their strong fragrances—are powerful medicine.

Examples:

- Peppermint (*Mentha piperita*)
- Lemon Balm (*Melissa officinalis*)
- Lavender (*Lavandula angustifolia*)
- Sage (*Salvia officinalis*)
- Oregano (*Origanum vulgare*)
- Thyme (*Thymus vulgaris*)

Key Traits:

- Square stems
- Opposite leaves (growing in pairs)
- Aromatic leaves and flowers
- Often purple or white blooms

Healing Actions:

- **Digestive**: Peppermint calms the gut and relieves gas.
- **Nervous system**: Lemon balm and lavender ease tension, anxiety, and insomnia.
- **Respiratory**: Thyme and sage act as expectorants and antiseptics.
- **Antimicrobial**: Oregano and thyme contain thymol and carvacrol—strong compounds that kill harmful microbes.

Caution:

- Excess peppermint may irritate those with acid reflux.
- Sage in high doses can be stimulating or neurotoxic due to thujone content—especially in essential oil form.

This family is an excellent starting point for those new to herbs. Their pleasant flavors and broad applications make them both versatile and safe in moderate doses.

Asteraceae — The Daisy Family

The daisy family (Asteraceae) is vast and filled with powerful medicinal allies. They often grow in disturbed soil and are common in meadows, lawns, and roadsides.

Examples:

- Chamomile (*Matricaria recutita*)
- Yarrow (*Achillea millefolium*)
- Calendula (*Calendula officinalis*)
- Echinacea (*Echinacea purpurea*)
- Dandelion (*Taraxacum officinale*)

Key Traits:

- Composite flowers (central disc + ray petals)
- Often bright yellow, white, or orange
- Milky or bitter sap in some species
- Taproot or fibrous roots

Healing Actions:

- **Anti-inflammatory**: Chamomile soothes both the gut and the mind.
- **Wound healing**: Calendula accelerates tissue repair and reduces infection.
- **Immune support**: Echinacea stimulates white blood cell production.
- **Digestive & liver support**: Dandelion supports bile flow, kidney cleansing, and skin detox.

Caution:

- People with ragweed allergies may react to Asteraceae herbs.
- Overuse of echinacea can overstimulate the immune system in autoimmune conditions.

Their diversity and resilience make these plants crucial in both first-aid kits and deep healing protocols.

Apiaceae — The Carrot Family

Also known as Umbelliferae, this family includes both culinary favorites and some of the most dangerous plants in North America. Their flowers grow in umbrella-like clusters called umbels.

Examples:

- Fennel (*Foeniculum vulgare*)
- Dill (*Anethum graveolens*)
- Angelica (*Angelica archangelica*)
- Cilantro (*Coriandrum sativum*)
- Parsley (*Petroselinum crispum*)

Key Traits:

- Umbel flower clusters
- Hollow stems
- Finely divided leaves (feathery)
- Aromatic seeds and roots

Healing Actions:

- **Carminative**: Fennel and dill reduce gas and soothe bloating.
- **Expectorant**: Angelica helps clear the lungs and loosens mucus.
- **Hormonal regulation**: Angelica supports reproductive health and relieves menstrual discomfort.
- **Detoxification**: Cilantro may bind to heavy metals and support detox pathways.

Critical Caution:

- This family contains deadly plants such as **Poison Hemlock** and **Water Hemlock**. NEVER wildcraft members of this family without absolute certainty of identification. These lookalikes can be fatal.

Herbs in this family offer a beautiful balance of taste and therapeutic power—but must be handled with knowledge and respect.

Malvaceae — The Mallow Family

The mallow family is deeply soothing. Its members produce mucilage—a slick, gooey compound that coats and calms inflamed or irritated tissue. They are often used where dryness or heat dominates the body.

Examples:

- Marshmallow (*Althaea officinalis*)
- Hibiscus (*Hibiscus sabdariffa*)
- Hollyhock (*Alcea rosea*)
- Okra (*Abelmoschus esculentus*)

Key Traits:

- Large, soft leaves
- Tall stems and showy flowers
- Slimy texture when chewed or steeped
- Edible roots, flowers, and leaves

Healing Actions:

- **Demulcent**: Marshmallow root soothes sore throats, dry coughs, and irritated gut linings.

- **Diuretic**: Hibiscus supports kidney and blood pressure balance.
- **Skin support**: Mallow leaves and flowers make excellent poultices for rashes and burns.

Caution:

- Because of their mucilage, they may delay absorption of pharmaceuticals—take herbs and medication separately.
- Excessive cooling can dampen digestion in those who are cold-natured.

These plants are gentle but incredibly effective. They're especially beneficial for the elderly, children, or those recovering from illness.

Identifying, Growing & Harvesting Herbs

Knowing what a plant is—and where, when, and how to gather or grow it—is what transforms interest into skill. This section focuses on real-world applications: identifying herbs, planting them with care, and harvesting them at their peak potency.

Plant Identification: Observation as a Discipline

You don't need to be a botanist to learn plant ID, but you do need to be observant. Here's how to start:

Clues to Examine:

- **Leaves:** Are they opposite or alternate? Smooth or serrated? What's their shape—lance, oval, heart, fan?
- **Stems:** Is it square (mint), hollow (carrot), hairy, or smooth?
- **Flowers:** Petal count? Symmetry? Color and scent? Umbel, spike, or cluster?
- **Smell:** Does it smell minty, sweet, sharp, or grassy when crushed?
- **Growth Pattern:** Solitary or clustered? Grows near water or on dry slopes?

Tools for Field Identification:

- Plant ID apps (PlantNet, Seek, iNaturalist)
- Regional field guides
- Hand lens and notebook
- Sketching or photo documentation

Warning: Some edible plants have poisonous lookalikes. Always use at least 2–3 trusted sources to confirm identification before using any wild plant.

Growing Herbs at Home

Home gardens are sacred spaces. Growing herbs fosters intimacy with plants and control over quality.

Essentials for Growing Success:

- **Sunlight**: Most herbs prefer 6–8 hours of direct sunlight.
- **Soil**: Loose, well-draining, slightly alkaline. Add compost regularly.
- **Water**: Deep but infrequent watering encourages root strength.
- **Spacing**: Proper airflow prevents mold and mildew.

Easy Herbs to Grow:

- **Chamomile**: Calming tea; self-seeds easily.
- **Peppermint**: Digestive aid; aggressive spreader—grow in pots.
- **Calendula**: Skin remedy; thrives in poor soil with full sun.
- **Holy Basil (Tulsi)**: Adaptogen; loves heat and consistent harvest.
- **Thyme**: Respiratory and antimicrobial; loves drier soil.
- **Lemon Balm**: Calming; partial shade and moist soil.

Ritual Tip: Speak to your plants. Touch them. Thank them. Herbalism is not just chemistry—it's relationship.

Harvesting & Drying

Proper harvesting ensures maximum potency and respect for the plant's cycle.

Best Times to Harvest:

- **Leaves:** Morning, before flowering
- **Flowers:** Mid-morning when fully open
- **Roots:** Late autumn or early spring
- **Seeds:** When dry but before wind dispersal

Drying Methods:

- Hang herbs in small bundles in a dark, airy place
- Dry petals on trays or screens
- Avoid ovens or sunlight which degrade oils
- Store in dark glass jars, tightly sealed, labeled with name and date

Shelf Life:

- Leaves & flowers: 1 year
- Roots & barks: 2–3 years
- Seeds: 2 years

Organic, Wildcrafted & Cultivated Herbs

How herbs are grown or gathered affects their quality, potency, and ecological footprint.

Organic Herbs

Certified organic herbs are grown without synthetic inputs and undergo inspections for quality and sustainability.

Advantages:

- Traceability
- Cleaner product for internal use
- Supports ethical farming

Disadvantages:

- Higher cost
- Certification doesn't guarantee freshness or potency—check scent, color, and texture

Wildcrafted Herbs

Wildcrafting means respectfully harvesting herbs from their native ecosystems. This method is spiritually rewarding—but also fraught with risk.

Advantages:

- Energetically vital and potent
- Grown in nature's own balance

Disadvantages:

- Risk of overharvesting
- No regulation or standardization
- Potential exposure to environmental toxins

Ethical Guidelines:

- Only harvest from abundant patches
- Leave at least 70% of any plant population untouched
- Avoid protected or endangered species
- Harvest away from roads, factories, or treated land

Cultivated Herbs

These are intentionally grown by gardeners or farms, with or without organic certification.

Advantages:

- Controllable environment
- Easy to reproduce
- Best for daily or culinary use

Disadvantages:

- May lack wild potency
- Subject to agricultural practices—ask about inputs

Sourcing Comparison Table

Type	Best For	Key Pros	Risks to Consider
Organic	Internal & family use	Certified, clean, safe	May be old, expensive
Wildcrafted	Ritual, advanced care	High energy, untamed	Overharvesting, contamination
Cultivated	Everyday use, beginners	Fresh, convenient	May lack standard potency

Final Thought...

Meeting your plant allies is a sacred initiation into a world that has always been waiting for you. As you walk the garden path, peer into hedgerows, or sip your hand-grown tea, you begin to remember what our ancestors never forgot: the plants are alive. They respond. They teach. And they heal.

By understanding families, learning to grow and harvest, and sourcing with awareness, you do more than make medicine. You make relationship. And that's where true healing begins.

PART II: THE WORKING APOTHECARY

Chapter 4

Tools of the Herbal Trade

"You don't need a fancy lab—just a few jars, a clean space, and the right intention."

Every good herbalist—whether working from a backyard garden or a kitchen counter—needs the right tools. But don't worry: building your herbal toolkit doesn't require a lot of money or a large workspace. Most of what you need is already in your home or can be found easily and affordably.

This chapter will guide you through setting up your herbal workspace, organizing your materials, and choosing the best liquids (called "carriers" or "solvents") to make herbal remedies like teas, tinctures, salves, and more.

Must-Have Herbal Equipment

You don't need a lot of tools to get started. Here are the basics:

- **Glass Jars** – Mason jars or clean, recycled jars with lids for making infusions, tinctures, and storing herbs.
- **Measuring Cups & Spoons** – For consistent and accurate recipes.
- **Funnels & Strainers** – Use stainless steel, nylon, or silicone for pouring and filtering.
- **Cheesecloth or Muslin** – Useful for straining out plant parts from liquids.
- **Mixing Bowls** – Choose glass or ceramic over plastic or metal for safe mixing.
- **Double Boiler** – Helps melt beeswax and oils gently without burning them.
- **Digital or Kitchen Scale** – For weighing herbs, especially when following specific recipes.
- **Labels & Markers** – Every jar or bottle should have a label with the name of the herb, date, and preparation method.

These tools make it easier to work cleanly, safely, and effectively.

Apothecary Storage & Organization

Good organization helps you stay inspired and prevents mistakes like using old herbs or mixing up ingredients.

Smart Storage Tips:

- **Use Glass Containers** – Store dried herbs in dark glass jars to block sunlight. Clear jars are okay if kept in a dark cabinet.
- **Keep It Cool & Dark** – Herbs last longer when stored away from heat and light. A shelf, box, or drawer works perfectly.
- **Label Everything** – Include the herb's name (common and Latin), date it was harvested or purchased, and what part of the plant it is (leaf, root, flower).
- **Track What You Have** – Use a notebook, binder, or digital spreadsheet to record what's in your apothecary and when it was made.

Clean, labeled, and organized tools show respect for the plants and help you become a more confident herbalist.

Choosing Your Carriers: Oils, Alcohols & More

When making remedies, the liquid you use to extract or apply the herb matters. This is called a **carrier** or **solvent**. It affects how strong the remedy will be and how the body absorbs it.

Oils – Used for skin remedies, massage blends, and infused oils.

- **Olive Oil** – Gentle, stable, and great for most uses.
- **Coconut Oil** – Solid at room temperature; good for balms and dry skin.
- **Sweet Almond or Jojoba Oil** – Light and non-greasy; excellent for face and hair.
- **Grapeseed or Sunflower Oil** – Absorbs quickly; perfect for massage.

Tip: Always use cold-pressed, food-grade oils.

Alcohol – Used to make tinctures (strong herbal extracts).

- **Vodka (80–100 proof)** – The most common tincture base. Safe, neutral taste.
- **Brandy or Rum** – Adds flavor and warmth; also effective.
- **Everclear (190 proof)** – Used for resins or very strong extractions, must be diluted.

Important: Only use drinking alcohol—never rubbing alcohol or denatured alcohol. They are toxic.

Vinegar & Glycerin – Alternatives to alcohol.

- **Apple Cider Vinegar** – Excellent for mineral-rich extractions and alcohol-free blends.
- **Vegetable Glycerin** – Sweet, thick, and great for children's or alcohol-sensitive formulas.

Vinegar and glycerin make milder remedies but are still effective with the right herbs.

Cleanliness & Safety

Always start with clean hands, clean tools, and a clean workspace. Sanitize glass jars and utensils with boiling water or a vinegar rinse. Dirty tools can ruin your remedy or introduce harmful bacteria.

- Wash and dry containers before and after each use.
- Store oils and alcohols tightly sealed to prevent oxidation or evaporation.
- Keep kids and pets out of your herbal workspace unless you're working together safely.

Final Thought...

You don't need a big studio or a huge investment to begin herbal crafting. A few clean jars, a spoon, a funnel, and a sense of curiosity are enough. Let your tools grow with you. As your skills expand, so will your apothecary. But remember: what matters most isn't the gear—it's your attention, your care, and your connection to the plants.

The best herbal remedies are made not just with tools, but with love, intention, and trust in nature.

Chapter 5

Core Herbs Every Home Should Have

This chapter is your trusted guide to building a personal apothecary—one that's simple, powerful, and deeply effective. These 40 herbs are chosen not for rarity or exotic flair, but for their reliability, safety, and usefulness in everyday situations.

Whether you're calming a child's stomach, easing a headache, boosting your immune system, or soothing a rash—these herbs have been loved and used by herbalists for generations.

We'll organize them by function, highlight how to combine them into blends, and guide you to trustworthy sources for purchasing. Most importantly, we'll share important safety tips so you feel confident using them at home.

Essential Herbal Profiles by Function

Nervous System Support

For calming and uplifting

1. Chamomile (*Matricaria recutita*)

Primary Actions: Nervine, anti-inflammatory, antispasmodic, mild sedative
Used For: Anxiety, insomnia, teething pain, bloating, menstrual cramps
Preparation: Tea (infusion), tincture, compress, bath
Caution: May trigger allergies in those sensitive to ragweed/daisy family

Features for Identification:
Dainty white petals with yellow button centers. Apple-like scent when crushed. Fern-like feathery leaves. Typically grows 6–12 inches tall with slender green stems.

2. Lemon Balm (*Melissa officinalis*)

Primary Actions: Calming, antiviral, carminative, mood-lifting
Used For: Restlessness, cold sores, digestive upset, mild depression
Preparation: Tea, tincture, infused oil
Caution: May affect thyroid with long-term heavy use

Features for Identification:
Heart-shaped, slightly crinkled leaves. Lemon scent when crushed. Square stems (mint family). Grows in dense green patches, 1–2 ft tall.

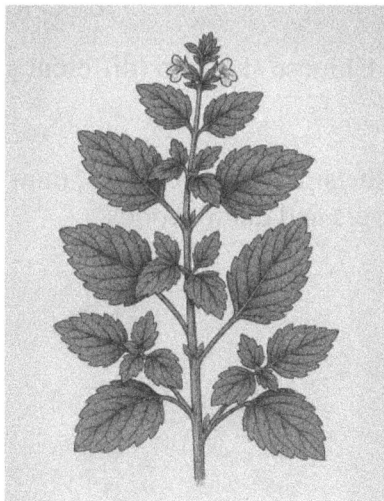

3. Lavender (*Lavandula angustifolia*)

Primary Actions: Relaxant, anti-inflammatory, antimicrobial
Used For: Stress, sleep, headaches, burns, bug bites

Preparation: Infused oil, tea, sachets, aromatherapy
Caution: Essential oil is strong—always dilute before skin use

Features for Identification:
Long grey-green leaves. Purple flower spikes on upright stems. Sweet floral scent. Woody base; thrives in dry, sunny climates.

4. Skullcap (*Scutellaria lateriflora*)

Primary Actions: Nervine, antispasmodic, anti-anxiety
Used For: Tension, insomnia, PMS, nerve twitching
Preparation: Tincture, tea
Caution: Do not confuse with Chinese skullcap (different species and action)

Features for Identification:
Small serrated leaves on opposite sides. Square stems, mint family. Tiny blue-purple hooded flowers. Found near rivers and damp woods.

5. Oatstraw (*Avena sativa*)

Primary Actions: Nervous system tonic, restorative, nourishing
Used For: Fatigue, adrenal burnout, anxiety, stress-related tension
Preparation: Long infusion (8+ hours), tincture
Caution: Avoid if allergic to oats

Features for Identification:
Grass-like stalks with oat seed heads. Milky sap (in "milky oats" stage). Soft green blades. Commonly grown in fields or gardens.

6. Peppermint (*Mentha piperita*)

Primary Actions: Carminative, cooling, antispasmodic, digestive
Used For: Gas, IBS, headaches, muscle tension
Preparation: Tea, tincture, essential oil (diluted)
Caution: Avoid if you have acid reflux or GERD

Features for Identification:
Dark green serrated leaves. Strong menthol aroma. Square stem (mint family). Grows rapidly, often spreads aggressively.

7. Ginger (*Zingiber officinale*)

Primary Actions: Warming, circulatory stimulant, anti-nausea
Used For: Motion sickness, cold limbs, menstrual cramps, poor digestion
Preparation: Decoction (boiled root), syrup, tincture, powder
Caution: Use caution with blood thinners or during hot conditions

Features for Identification:
Rhizome (underground root) is the usable part. Pale green shoots with yellow-green flowers. Tropical climates only (grow indoors in pots elsewhere). Spicy, sharp aroma when cut.

8. Fennel (*Foeniculum vulgare*)

Primary Actions: Carminative, anti-gas, galactagogue
Used For: Bloating, colic (babies), gas, poor milk supply

Preparation: Crushed seeds as tea, tincture
Caution: Mild estrogenic effects—avoid in hormone-sensitive conditions

Features for Identification:
Feathery, dill-like leaves. Umbrella-shaped yellow flowers. Tall hollow stalks. Licorice-like aroma from crushed seeds.

9. Dandelion Root (*Taraxacum officinale*)

Primary Actions: Liver tonic, digestive bitter, diuretic
Used For: Acne, sluggish digestion, water retention, PMS
Preparation: Roasted or raw decoction, tincture
Caution: Can interfere with lithium or potassium-sparing diuretics

Features for Identification:
Jagged leaves in a rosette pattern. Hollow stem with white sap. Bright yellow flower heads. Deep taproot—harvest in fall for best potency.

10. Slippery Elm (*Ulmus rubra*)

Primary Actions: Demulcent, soothing, anti-inflammatory
Used For: Acid reflux, sore throats, IBS, ulcers
Preparation: Powder mixed with water/honey, lozenges
Caution: May delay absorption of meds—space doses

Features for Identification:
Tall tree with rough, reddish-brown bark. Inner bark is soft and mucilaginous. Elliptic, serrated leaves. Bark harvested sustainably from deadfall only (wild population sensitive).

Immune & Respiratory Support

For boosting defenses, easing colds, and soothing coughs

11. Echinacea (*Echinacea purpurea*)

Primary Actions: Immune stimulant, antiviral, lymphatic
Used For: Colds, flu, swollen glands, infections, wound healing
Preparation: Tincture, decoction, capsule
Caution: Avoid long-term use if you have autoimmune conditions

Features for Identification:
Purple daisy-like flowers with a raised cone center. Rough, lance-shaped leaves. Strong central stem. Common in garden beds and meadows.

12. Elderberry (*Sambucus nigra*)

Primary Actions: Antiviral, immune-boosting, antioxidant
Used For: Cold and flu prevention, fever, inflammation
Preparation: Syrup, tincture, tea, gummies
Caution: Raw berries and stems can cause nausea—always cook or prepare properly

Features for Identification:
Clusters of dark purple-black berries. Flat-topped white flower heads. Compound serrated leaves. Grows as a small tree or large shrub.

13. Mullein (*Verbascum thapsus*)

Primary Actions: Lung tonic, expectorant, demulcent
Used For: Dry cough, bronchitis, asthma, chest tightness
Preparation: Tea (strained well), tincture, infused oil
Caution: Fine leaf hairs may irritate—always strain tea with cheesecloth

Features for Identification:
Tall stalk with yellow flowers. Large, soft, woolly leaves. Rosette base in first year.
Found in dry, sunny fields.

14. Thyme (*Thymus vulgaris*)

Primary Actions: Antimicrobial, antifungal, expectorant, digestive
Used For: Wet coughs, colds, lung infections, digestion
Preparation: Tea, tincture, infused oil, steam
Caution: Use essential oil only diluted—very strong internally

Features for Identification:
Tiny rounded leaves with intense aroma. Woody stems. Small purple flowers. Grows low
and bushy.

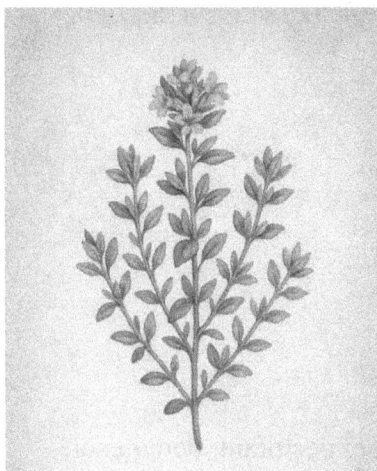

15. Yarrow (*Achillea millefolium*)

Primary Actions: Anti-inflammatory, astringent, diaphoretic
Used For: Fevers, wounds, menstrual pain, skin irritation
Preparation: Tea, tincture, compress, salve
Caution: Related to ragweed—may cause allergies in sensitive individuals

Features for Identification:
Fern-like feathery leaves. Flat flower clusters (white or pink). Strong, aromatic scent. Common in open fields and roadsides.

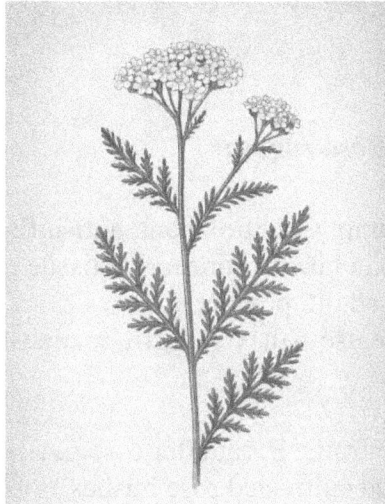

16. Elecampane (*Inula helenium*)

Primary Actions: Expectorant, antimicrobial, warming
Used For: Deep lung congestion, chronic bronchitis, wet coughs
Preparation: Decoction, syrup, tincture
Caution: Use with caution in pregnancy; bitter taste may cause nausea in sensitive people

Features for Identification:
Tall plant (3–6 feet). Broad fuzzy leaves. Large yellow daisy-like flowers. Root is the medicinal part.

17. Rose Hips (*Rosa canina*, *Rosa rugosa*)

Primary Actions: Rich in vitamin C, antioxidant, anti-inflammatory
Used For: Immune support, skin health, connective tissue repair
Preparation: Syrup, tea, infused oil, powder
Caution: Remove seeds before use—they can irritate digestive tract

Features for Identification:
Bright red or orange berry-like fruits. Form after rose petals fall. Round or oval with smooth skin. Found on wild and cultivated rose bushes.

18. Usnea (*Usnea spp.*)

Primary Actions: Antibacterial, antifungal, immune-enhancing
Used For: Respiratory infections, skin infections, sore throats

Preparation: Tincture (alcohol extract only), salve
Caution: Do not harvest from polluted areas—lichen absorbs toxins

Features for Identification:
Lichen that grows like pale green "beard" from tree branches. Elastic white inner core when pulled. Common on old hardwoods.

19. Nettle (*Urtica dioica*)

Primary Actions: Mineral-rich, anti-inflammatory, antihistamine
Used For: Allergies, joint pain, anemia, urinary support
Preparation: Tea, tincture, cooked greens
Caution: Fresh plant stings—handle with gloves; stings disappear when cooked or dried

Features for Identification:
Serrated, heart-shaped leaves. Fine hairs on stems and leaves. Square stem. Grows in rich, moist soils.

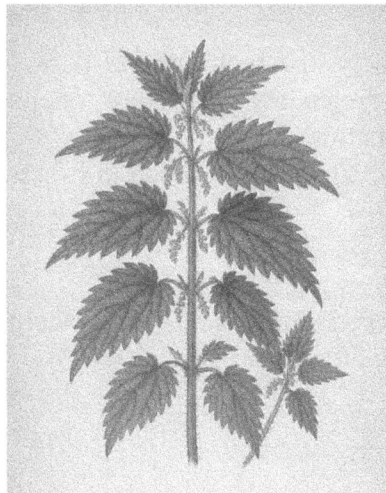

20. Calendula (*Calendula officinalis*)

Primary Actions: Anti-inflammatory, skin healing, antimicrobial
Used For: Cuts, burns, rashes, yeast infections, lymph support
Preparation: Infused oil, salve, tea, tincture
Caution: May trigger allergy in those sensitive to the daisy family

Features for Identification:
Bright orange or yellow daisy-like blooms. Sticky, slightly fuzzy leaves. Edible petals. Common in garden beds.

Women's Wellness, Hormonal Support & Skin Healing

21. Raspberry Leaf (*Rubus idaeus*)

Primary Actions: Uterine tonic, astringent, mineral-rich
Used For: Menstrual cramps, pregnancy prep, labor tone, postpartum healing
Preparation: Tea, infusion, tincture
Caution: Safe during pregnancy, but best avoided in first trimester unless guided by a professional

Features for Identification:
Soft, pale-green undersides on serrated leaves. Thorny stems. White flowers that turn into raspberries. Found in bramble patches.

22. Vitex (Chaste Tree Berry) (*Vitex agnus-castus*)

Primary Actions: Hormone-balancing, pituitary modulator, PMS support
Used For: Irregular cycles, PMS, menopause, low progesterone
Preparation: Tincture, capsule
Caution: Not recommended during pregnancy. May take 2–3 months to notice effects.

Features for Identification:
Shrub with long spikes of purple flowers. Leaves are palmate (like fingers). Small, dark brown berries in fall. Mediterranean in origin but cultivated worldwide.

23. Motherwort (*Leonurus cardiaca*)

Primary Actions: Nervine, antispasmodic, uterine tonic, heart-supportive
Used For: Menstrual tension, palpitations from anxiety, PMS anger
Preparation: Tincture, tea (bitter!)
Caution: Avoid in pregnancy; may stimulate uterine contractions

Features for Identification:
Lobed leaves with toothed edges. Square stems, small pink-purple fuzzy flowers. Grows 3–5 ft tall; smells strong and earthy.

24. Red Clover (*Trifolium pratense*)

Primary Actions: Lymphatic, estrogenic, detoxifying, nourishing
Used For: Menopausal support, detox, lymph congestion, skin eruptions
Preparation: Tea, tincture, poultice
Caution: Mild estrogenic effects—consult professional for hormone-sensitive conditions

Features for Identification:
Round pink-purple flower heads. Trifoliate (3-part) oval leaves with a pale "V" marking. Common in fields and pastures.

25. Marshmallow Root (*Althaea officinalis*)

Primary Actions: Demulcent, moistening, anti-inflammatory
Used For: Dry throat, cough, UTI, ulcers, dry skin
Preparation: Cold infusion (root), tea, syrup
Caution: May reduce absorption of medications—take separately by 1 hour

Features for Identification:
Tall plant with soft, broad velvety leaves. Light pink-white hibiscus-like flowers. Grows well in moist gardens or riverbanks.

26. Comfrey (*Symphytum officinale*)

Primary Actions: Cell proliferant, tissue healing, anti-inflammatory
Used For: Bruises, sprains, broken bones, deep wounds (external use only)
Preparation: Salve, poultice, infused oil
Caution: Do *not* use internally—contains pyrrolizidine alkaloids harmful to the liver. Avoid on deep wounds that haven't been cleaned.

Features for Identification:
Large hairy leaves. Bell-shaped purple flowers. Thick, deep roots. Found in moist soil or along rivers.

27. Plantain Leaf (*Plantago major / lanceolata*)

Primary Actions: Drawing, cooling, anti-inflammatory, antimicrobial
Used For: Bug bites, splinters, cuts, boils, sore throats
Preparation: Poultice (chewed or mashed), tea, tincture
Caution: Safe; no known risks

Features for Identification:
Broad (or narrow) ribbed leaves growing in ground-level rosettes. Long fibrous veins. Found in cracks of sidewalks, fields, and lawns.

28. St. John's Wort (*Hypericum perforatum*)

Primary Actions: Antiviral, mood-lifting, nerve soothing, wound-healing
Used For: Mild depression, nerve pain, cold sores, sunburns
Preparation: Tincture, infused oil, capsules

Caution: Interacts with MANY medications—antidepressants, birth control, blood thinners. Avoid with those. Increases sun sensitivity.

Features for Identification:
Bright yellow five-petaled flowers with red oil glands. Leaves show tiny perforations when held to light. Grows along roadsides and meadows.

29. Chickweed (*Stellaria media*)

Primary Actions: Cooling, anti-itch, demulcent, lymph-moving
Used For: Rashes, eczema, pink eye, minor wounds, skin irritation
Preparation: Poultice, tea, infused oil, salve
Caution: Spoils quickly when fresh—use or preserve promptly

Features for Identification:
Small green leaves in pairs. Tiny white star-like flowers. Weak sprawling stems with one line of hair. Grows in moist, shady areas.

30. Burdock Root (*Arctium lappa*)

Primary Actions: Liver-supporting, lymphatic, skin-cleansing
Used For: Acne, eczema, sluggish digestion, inflammation
Preparation: Decoction, tincture, food (peel and cook root)
Caution: May lower blood sugar—monitor in diabetics

Features for Identification:
Huge heart-shaped leaves. Purple thistle-like burrs. Long deep taproot. Found in wild meadows, ditches, and disturbed ground.

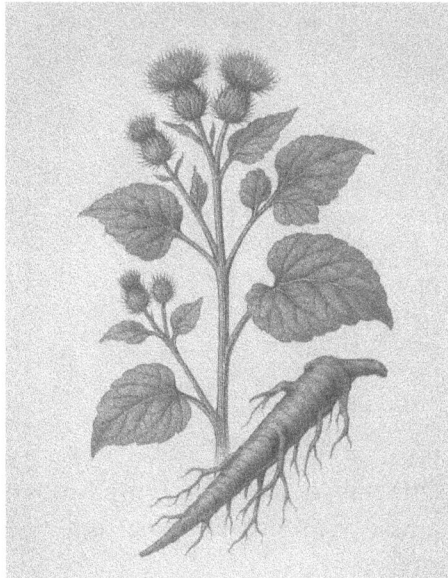

Family First Aid & Gentle Everyday Remedies

For home use with kids, elderly, and sensitive constitutions

31. Catnip (*Nepeta cataria*)

Primary Actions: Nervine, carminative, antispasmodic, mild sedative
Used For: Colic, restlessness in children, fevers, gas, teething
Preparation: Tea, tincture, bath
Caution: Very safe; no known risks—may excite cats, though!

Features for Identification:
Heart-shaped, fuzzy gray-green leaves. Square stem (mint family). Small pale purple-white flowers. Strong musky-mint scent when crushed.

32. Spearmint (*Mentha spicata*)

Primary Actions: Cooling, digestive, slightly uplifting
Used For: Mild digestive upset, headaches, morning sickness
Preparation: Tea, tincture, infused water
Caution: Gentler than peppermint—better for children and pregnant women

Features for Identification:
Pointed, sharply serrated leaves. Square stems. Sweeter, softer scent than peppermint. Grows quickly in sun or partial shade.

33. Lemon Verbena (*Aloysia citrodora*)

Primary Actions: Nervine, uplifting, calming, carminative
Used For: Anxiety, grief, insomnia, poor appetite
Preparation: Tea (fresh or dried), tincture, infused honey
Caution: Safe; no known toxicity

Features for Identification:
Slender lance-shaped leaves. Very strong lemon scent. Small white or lilac flower clusters. Woody stemmed shrub in warm climates.

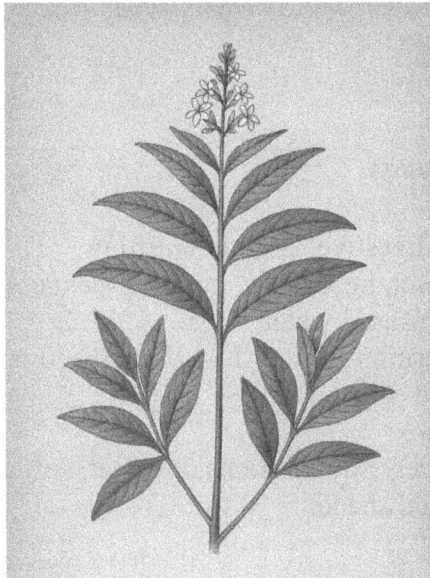

34. Licorice Root (*Glycyrrhiza glabra*)

Primary Actions: Demulcent, anti-inflammatory, adrenal tonic, harmonizer
Used For: Cough, sore throat, ulcers, adrenal fatigue
Preparation: Decoction, tincture, powder
Caution: Avoid long-term or high doses with high blood pressure or during pregnancy

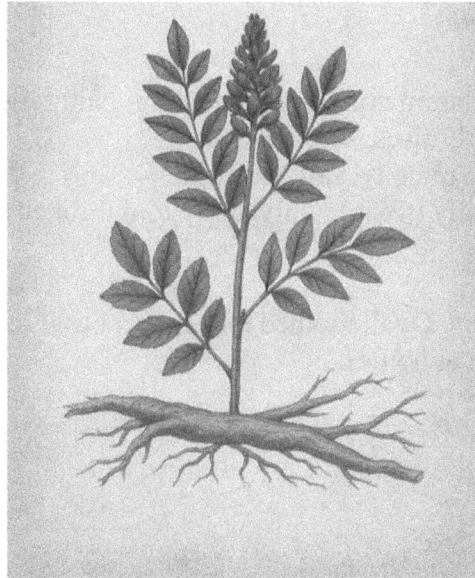

Features for Identification:
Long sweet-tasting roots. Compound pinnate leaves. Purple flowers. Rarely found wild; mostly cultivated in warm climates.

35. Holy Basil (Tulsi) *(Ocimum sanctum)*

Primary Actions: Adaptogen, anti-stress, immune-supportive
Used For: Anxiety, fatigue, cold prevention, foggy thinking
Preparation: Tea, tincture, infused ghee or honey
Caution: Avoid during pregnancy unless advised professionally

Features for Identification:
Fragrant purple or green leaves. Slightly serrated with square stem. Grows like common basil but more pungent.

36. Arnica *(Arnica montana)*

Primary Actions: Anti-inflammatory, bruise-healing, pain relief (external use only)
Used For: Sprains, strains, bruises, sore muscles
Preparation: Homeopathic remedy, salve, compress
Caution: Never use internally (toxic). Only apply to unbroken skin.

Features for Identification:
Golden-yellow daisy flowers. Oval, toothed leaves in a basal rosette. Found in alpine meadows (not easily grown at home).

37. Garlic *(Allium sativum)*

Primary Actions: Antibacterial, antiviral, circulatory stimulant, immune-boosting
Used For: Infections, colds, cough, high blood pressure
Preparation: Raw, cooked, infused in oil (topical), syrup
Caution: Can irritate stomach in sensitive individuals. Raw use may cause body odor.

Features for Identification:
Bulb of many cloves. Long flat green leaves. Strong pungent aroma. Grows well in most gardens from cloves.

38. Sage (*Salvia officinalis*)

Primary Actions: Antimicrobial, drying, cognitive support
Used For: Sore throat, hot flashes, excess sweating, memory support
Preparation: Tea, tincture, gargle, smoke bundle
Caution: Avoid high doses in pregnancy; may reduce lactation

Features for Identification:
Silvery, fuzzy leaves. Woody base. Purple-blue flower spikes. Aromatic, savory scent when crushed.

39. Rosemary (*Rosmarinus officinalis*)

Primary Actions: Circulatory stimulant, antioxidant, memory-enhancing
Used For: Brain fog, poor circulation, hair groewth, fatigue

Preparation: Tea, infused oil, tincture, culinary
Caution: Avoid strong oil in epilepsy; may be too stimulating before bed

Features for Identification:
Needle-like green leaves with white underside. Woody shrub with blue flowers. Sharp, piney scent.

40. Blue Vervain (*Verbena hastata*)

Primary Actions: Nervine, liver-supportive, cooling, tension-releasing
Used For: Overwhelm, stress in the shoulders/neck, PMS, restlessness
Preparation: Tincture (very bitter), tea
Caution: Strong in energy; avoid use during pregnancy

Features for Identification:
Tall wildflower with branching spikes of small purple-blue flowers. Leaves are narrow, toothed, and rough. Often found near wetlands.

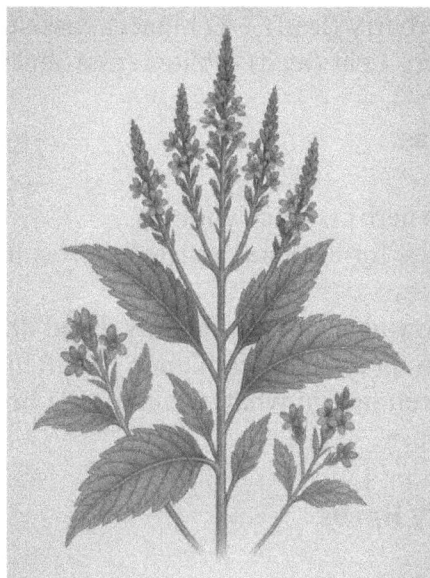

Combining Herbs into Effective Blends

Making herbal formulas is like building a supportive team—each herb plays a role. When combined thoughtfully, herbs work together to offer a more balanced and effective result than one herb alone.

Here's a simple framework:

1. Choose a Primary Herb (The "Lead")

This is the herb that directly addresses the main issue you're treating.
Example: For anxiety, you might choose **Lemon Balm** as your lead.

2. Add a Supporting Herb (The "Assistant")

This herb strengthens or complements the action of the lead herb.
Example: **Chamomile** or **Skullcap** can enhance Lemon Balm's relaxing effect.

3. Include a Catalyst Herb (The "Mover")

This herb helps circulate the remedy throughout the body and improves absorption. These are often aromatic or warming herbs like **Ginger**, **Licorice**, or **Peppermint**.

Sample Blends:

- **Sleep Support**: Chamomile (lead) + Skullcap (assistant) + Lavender (catalyst)
- **Digestion Ease**: Fennel (lead) + Ginger (assistant) + Peppermint (catalyst)

- **Immune Boost**: Elderberry (lead) + Echinacea (assistant) + Ginger (catalyst)
- **PMS Relief**: Raspberry Leaf (lead) + Vitex (assistant) + Lemon Balm (catalyst)

Tips for Successful Formulas:

- Keep it simple. Three herbs is often enough.
- Use roughly equal parts for lead and assistant herbs; half a part or less for the catalyst.
- Taste matters! No one wants a medicine they dread drinking. Use naturally tasty herbs like lemon balm, licorice, or cinnamon to soften bitter ones.
- Always record what you use, in what amounts, and how it worked. That's how herbalists learn and grow.

Where to Buy High-Quality Herbs

Not all herbs on the market are created equal. To make effective, safe remedies, you need herbs that are **fresh, potent, clean, and responsibly grown or harvested**.

What to Look For:

- **Color**: Herbs should still look vibrant. Green should be green—not brown or gray.
- **Scent**: Herbs should have a strong, pleasant aroma. Faded scent = faded potency.
- **Feel**: Dried herbs shouldn't crumble to dust. They should still feel alive, slightly springy, or at least intact.
- **Labels**: Quality packaging will tell you the plant's name (common & Latin), part used, origin, and harvest or expiration date.

Trusted Herb Suppliers:

United States:

- *Mountain Rose Herbs* – Excellent quality, certified organic
- *Starwest Botanicals* – Good for bulk herbs
- *Frontier Co-op* – Widely available and affordable
- *Pacific Botanicals* – Great for fresh roots and rare plants

United Kingdom:

- *Indigo Herbs* – Organic, well-packaged, extensive inventory
- *Baldwins* – Historic London apothecary with strong reputation

Elsewhere:

- Seek out *local herbalists, farmers markets*, or *community apothecaries* for fresh, ethical sources.

Certifications to Look For:

- Certified Organic
- Ethically Wildcrafted
- Non-Irradiated (herbs processed with light to kill bacteria often lose potency)
- Fair Trade and Local where possible

Cautions When Purchasing Herbs

- Avoid dusty herbs in clear bulk bins exposed to sunlight and air—they may have lost their strength.
- Be cautious with online marketplaces that don't list sourcing, certifications, or expiration dates.
- Imported herbs (especially roots or barks) should be tested for heavy metals or pesticide residue.
- Always smell and inspect your herbs. Trust your senses—if it looks and smells lifeless, it probably is.

Final Words…

Your herbal shelf doesn't need to be stocked with 200 jars to be powerful. With these 40 herbs, you can meet most everyday needs with skill and heart. Use this chapter as a guide, not just for shopping, but for **building relationships with your plants**—one blend, one brew, and one beautiful jar at a time.

Chapter 6

Creating Your Herbal Healing Space

"A well-loved apothecary is not just a shelf of jars—it's a sacred space where healing begins."

Creating your herbal healing space doesn't mean you need an entire room or a fancy cabinet. It simply means carving out a place—however small—where your herbs live, your tools rest, and your practice feels intentional.

Whether it's a corner of your kitchen, a rolling cart near a window, or a reclaimed shelf in your hallway, this space becomes more than just storage. It becomes a relationship—a daily invitation to reconnect with the plants and your healing work.

How to Store, Organize, and Rotate Herbs

Proper storage is one of the easiest ways to preserve your herbs' strength and shelf life. Herbs that are exposed to light, heat, air, or moisture lose potency quickly. But with a few simple choices, you can create an apothecary that's both beautiful and functional.

Storage Basics:

- **Containers**: Use airtight glass jars—preferably dark (amber or cobalt blue). If using clear jars, keep them inside cabinets or covered boxes to avoid light exposure.
- **Labels**: Every jar should be labeled with:
    - Common and botanical name
    - Part used (leaf, root, flower, etc.)
    - Date harvested or purchased
    - Source (especially if wildcrafted or homegrown)
- **Location**: Store your jars in a cool, dark place—away from stoves, sinks, and sunny windows.
- **Rotation**: Check your herbs every 6–12 months. Smell them, look at their color, and discard anything that's lost its scent or vibrancy. Compost old herbs—they've done their job.

Tip: Build a "Herbs to Use Soon" basket or tray. This keeps older stock visible and encourages regular use before it expires.

Keeping an Herbal Journal or Inventory

One of the most overlooked but valuable tools for any herbalist is a good **herbal journal**. It becomes a living record of what you've learned, tried, created, and discovered along the way.

What to Include in Your Journal:

- Notes on each herb's effects on you or family members
- Recipes you've tried (and how they turned out)
- Formulas you've created or adjusted
- Blends that worked well—and those that didn't
- New herbs you want to try
- Dates for when remedies were made and when they should be discarded

An herbal journal helps you grow in confidence and memory. It also serves as a personal guidebook tailored to your body, your climate, and your style.

Inventory Sheet Ideas:

- List all herbs you currently have, including quantity and purchase/harvest date
- Track tinctures, oils, salves, teas, and syrups
- Add a "needs restocking" column to stay organized

Bonus: Over time, you'll notice which herbs you reach for most often. These are your "core allies"—the herbs you should always keep stocked.

PART III: REMEDY CRAFTING & FORMULAS

Chapter 7

Herbal Teas That Heal: Blends & Rituals

"When hot water meets a healing plant, something ancient awakens."

Herbal teas—or **tisanes**—are among the gentlest, safest, and most traditional forms of herbal medicine. For thousands of years, people across the globe have brewed herbs into hot water to support healing, soothe the spirit, and nourish the body. With no need for fancy tools or complicated techniques, teas provide an incredibly accessible and soul-nourishing way to incorporate herbs into your daily life.

Whether you're looking to ease a stomachache, calm a racing mind, strengthen immunity, or mark a meaningful moment in your day, **a cup of herbal tea can meet you where you are**. It becomes more than a remedy—it becomes ritual.

This chapter will guide you through the **right ways to prepare medicinal teas**, how to **incorporate them into your daily rhythm**, and offer **35 therapeutic recipes** for common concerns. Each formula includes **dosage suggestions and important precautions**, so you can sip with confidence and care.

How to Brew Medicinal Teas

Not all teas are brewed the same. If your goal is therapeutic value—not just flavor—you'll need to pay close attention to **herbal parts** and **preparation methods**. Here's a quick guide:

Infusions – for leaves, flowers, and soft aerial parts

- Pour boiling water over the herbs
- Cover to trap volatile oils
- Steep for **10–20 minutes**
- Strain and drink warm

Decoctions – for roots, bark, seeds, and tough stems

- Add herbs to cold water in a pot
- Simmer gently for **15–30 minutes**
- Strain and sip slowly

General Dosage Guidelines:

- **1–2 teaspoons** dried herb (or 1 tablespoon fresh) per 8 oz of water
- For chronic conditions, drink **2–3 cups daily**, in divided doses
- Children, elderly, or sensitive individuals: **start with half** the adult amount

Always brew your tea fresh, cover during steeping, and drink it mindfully. Teas can be sweetened with honey or mellowed with lemon if needed.

Daily Rituals & Wellness Brews

Herbal teas become more potent when you **make them part of a daily rhythm**. A morning brew can awaken your senses, a midday infusion can refocus your mind, and an evening tea can guide your body into restful sleep.

Here are a few examples of **rituals you can weave into your day**:

- **Morning Awakening**: Try a cup of Tulsi and Lemongrass to greet the day with clarity and grounded energy. Light a candle, set an intention, and breathe deeply as the steam rises.
- **Midday Reset**: Brew Peppermint and Fennel to ease digestive heaviness after lunch, especially during busy days.
- **Evening Unwind**: Sip Chamomile, Lavender, and Skullcap to ease mental chatter and cue your nervous system to rest.

You can also make **seasonal tea traditions**—like elderberry and cinnamon in winter for immune defense, or hibiscus and mint in summer for cooling relief. Let your body guide you. Over time, your tea blends become a mirror of your needs.

35 Herbal Tea Recipes by Ailment

The heart of this chapter is a collection of **35 functional tea blends**, designed for everyday wellness challenges—from stress and sleep to colds, cramps, and clarity. Each recipe includes:

- **Precise ratios** (by teaspoon or tablespoon)
- **Preparation method**
- **Dosage guidelines**
- **Safety cautions**
- **Who should avoid it (if applicable)**

These teas are gentle but powerful, crafted to be both effective and easy to make with herbs you can grow, forage, or buy easily.

1. Calm Clarity Tea (For Anxiety + Mental Restlessness)

Ingredients:

- 1 tsp Lemon Balm
- 1 tsp Chamomile
- ½ tsp Lavender

Preparation: Infuse in 1 cup boiling water for 10–15 minutes, covered. Strain and sip warm.

Dosage: 1 cup up to 3 times daily.

Caution: Avoid Lemon Balm in cases of hypothyroidism.

2. Peaceful Sleep Blend

Ingredients:

- 1 tsp Skullcap
- 1 tsp Chamomile
- ½ tsp Lavender

Preparation: Infuse in 1 cup just-boiled water for 15 minutes. Strain before bed.

Dosage: 1 cup 30–60 minutes before sleep.

Caution: Do not combine with sedative medications unless advised.

3. Gentle Child's Sleep Tea

Ingredients:

- 1 tsp Chamomile
- ½ tsp Lemon Balm
- ½ tsp Catnip

Preparation: Infuse in 1 cup hot water for 10 minutes. Strain well.

Dosage: ½ cup for children over 2 years; 1 cup for older children/adults.

Caution: Test for allergies with daisy family (chamomile). Always supervise children.

4. Belly Ease Blend (For Bloating + Gas)

Ingredients:

- 1 tsp Peppermint
- 1 tsp Fennel
- ½ tsp Lemon Balm

Preparation: Infuse in hot water for 10 minutes. Cover and strain.

Dosage: 1 cup after meals or at first sign of discomfort.

Caution: Avoid Peppermint in cases of reflux or GERD.

5. Menstrual Soothe Tea

Ingredients:

- 1 tsp Raspberry Leaf
- 1 tsp Chamomile
- ½ tsp Ginger

Preparation: Infuse Raspberry and Chamomile in boiling water. Add Ginger as decoction or powder.

Dosage: 1–2 cups per day during menstruation.

Caution: Avoid high-dose Ginger if on blood thinners.

6. Immune Defense Brew

Ingredients:

- 1 tsp Elderberry
- 1 tsp Echinacea
- ½ tsp Ginger

Preparation: Simmer Elderberry and Echinacea in 2 cups water for 15 minutes. Add Ginger, simmer 5 more. Strain and sweeten if desired.

Dosage: 1 cup up to 3x/day at onset of illness.

Caution: Avoid Echinacea in autoimmune conditions. Never use raw Elderberry.

7. Throat Soothing Tea

Ingredients:

- 1 tsp Slippery Elm (powder)
- 1 tsp Marshmallow Root
- ½ tsp Licorice Root

Preparation: Cold infusion: Combine herbs with room-temp water. Steep 4–6 hours or overnight. Strain.

Dosage: Sip ½ cup every few hours.

Caution: Licorice may raise blood pressure in large amounts.

8. Anti-Allergy Spring Tea

Ingredients:

- 1 tsp Nettle Leaf
- 1 tsp Red Clover
- ½ tsp Peppermint

Preparation: Infuse in 1 cup just-boiled water for 15 minutes. Strain and sip.

Dosage: 2–3 cups per day during allergy season.

Caution: Red Clover is mildly estrogenic; avoid with hormone-sensitive conditions.

9. Focus & Energy Tea

Ingredients:

- 1 tsp Holy Basil (Tulsi)
- ½ tsp Rosemary
- ½ tsp Lemon Balm

Preparation: Infuse in 1 cup boiling water for 10 minutes. Strain.

Dosage: 1–2 cups daily in the morning or early afternoon.

Caution: Avoid Rosemary if you have epilepsy or are pregnant.

10. Cramps + Calm Blend

Ingredients:

- 1 tsp Motherwort
- 1 tsp Raspberry Leaf
- ½ tsp Chamomile

Preparation: Infuse all herbs in 1 cup boiling water for 15 minutes. Strain and serve warm.

Dosage: 1–2 cups daily before and during menstruation.

Caution: Avoid Motherwort during pregnancy.

11. Winter Wellness Tea (Immune Boosting)

Ingredients:

- 1 tsp Elderberry
- 1 tsp Ginger Root
- ½ tsp Licorice Root

Preparation: Simmer herbs in 2 cups water for 20 minutes. Strain.

Dosage: 1 cup twice daily during cold/flu season.

Caution: Avoid Licorice with high blood pressure; never use raw Elderberry.

12. Lung Support Decoction

Ingredients:

- 1 tsp Mullein Leaf
- 1 tsp Elecampane Root
- ½ tsp Licorice Root

Preparation: Simmer all herbs in water for 25 minutes. Strain through cheesecloth (especially for Mullein fuzz).

Dosage: 1 cup, 2–3 times per day during cough or congestion.

Caution: Do not use Elecampane during pregnancy. Strain Mullein well to avoid irritation.

13. Allergy Defense Blend

Ingredients:

- 1 tsp Nettle Leaf
- 1 tsp Red Clover
- ½ tsp Peppermint

Preparation: Infuse in hot water for 15 minutes, covered.

Dosage: 1 cup, up to 3 times daily during allergy season.

Caution: Red Clover may affect estrogen; avoid in hormone-sensitive conditions.

14. Liver Cleanse Tea

Ingredients:

- 1 tsp Dandelion Root
- 1 tsp Burdock Root
- ½ tsp Ginger

Preparation: Simmer all herbs in 2 cups water for 20–25 minutes. Strain.

Dosage: 1 cup per day for 1–2 weeks during spring/fall detox.

Caution: Monitor if on diuretics or diabetic medication (Burdock can lower blood sugar).

15. Inflammation Easer

Ingredients:

- 1 tsp Ginger Root
- 1 tsp Calendula Flowers
- ½ tsp Red Clover

Preparation: Infuse Calendula and Red Clover in hot water; decoct Ginger separately and mix.

Dosage: 1–2 cups per day as needed.

Caution: Monitor Licorice or Red Clover effects if on hormonal therapy or meds.

16. Cold Season Rescue

Ingredients:

- 1 tsp Yarrow
- 1 tsp Elderflower (or Elderberry)
- ½ tsp Peppermint

Preparation: Infuse in hot water for 15 minutes, covered.

Dosage: 1 cup at first sign of a cold, then every 4–6 hours.

Caution: Yarrow may cause allergic reactions in people sensitive to the daisy family.

17. Joint Relief Tea

Ingredients:

- 1 tsp Nettle Leaf
- 1 tsp Burdock Root
- ½ tsp Ginger

Preparation: Simmer Burdock and Ginger for 20 minutes; steep Nettle separately and combine.

Dosage: 1 cup, twice daily during flare-ups.

Caution: Nettle is drying; counter with demulcents if needed.

18. Fever Tea (Diaphoretic Blend)

Ingredients:

- 1 tsp Yarrow
- 1 tsp Elderflower
- ½ tsp Lemon Balm

Preparation: Steep in hot water, covered, for 15 minutes. Sip hot while wrapped in a blanket.

Dosage: 1 cup every 2–3 hours during fever onset.

Caution: Avoid with ragweed allergy (Yarrow).

19. Skin Clarity Tea (For Acne + Detox)

Ingredients:

- 1 tsp Red Clover
- 1 tsp Burdock Root
- ½ tsp Calendula

Preparation: Simmer Burdock; infuse Red Clover and Calendula. Combine.

Dosage: 1 cup daily for 2–3 weeks.

Caution: Avoid Red Clover with hormone therapy.

20. Mucus Melt Tea (Respiratory Mover)

Ingredients:

- 1 tsp Thyme
- 1 tsp Elecampane
- ½ tsp Licorice

Preparation: Simmer all herbs for 20 minutes. Strain well.

Dosage: ½ to 1 cup every 4 hours during thick, wet cough.

Caution: Not for pregnancy; monitor Licorice if hypertensive.

21. Energy Lift Tea

Ingredients:

- 1 tsp Holy Basil
- 1 tsp Peppermint
- ½ tsp Ginger

Preparation: Steep Holy Basil and Peppermint. Simmer Ginger separately and combine.

Dosage: 1 cup in the morning or mid-afternoon.

Caution: May be overstimulating for sensitive individuals; avoid close to bedtime.

---

22. Focus + Memory Brew

Ingredients:

- 1 tsp Rosemary
- 1 tsp Lemon Balm
- ½ tsp Holy Basil

Preparation: Infuse all herbs in hot water for 10–15 minutes.

Dosage: 1 cup in the morning for clarity.

Caution: Rosemary may overstimulate in high doses or in epilepsy.

---

23. Grief & Emotional Support Tea

Ingredients:

- 1 tsp Lemon Balm
- 1 tsp Lavender
- ½ tsp Motherwort

Preparation: Steep in hot water for 15 minutes, covered.

Dosage: 1 cup 1–3x daily during periods of sadness or loss.

Caution: Avoid Motherwort during pregnancy.

24. Adrenal Nourishment Blend

Ingredients:

- 1 tsp Oatstraw
- 1 tsp Nettle
- ½ tsp Licorice Root

Preparation: Steep Oatstraw and Nettle; decoct Licorice and combine.

Dosage: 1 cup daily over several weeks.

Caution: Avoid Licorice with hypertension.

25. Menopause Soother

Ingredients:

- 1 tsp Red Clover
- 1 tsp Sage
- ½ tsp Lemon Balm

Preparation: Infuse in hot water, covered, for 15 minutes.

Dosage: 1–2 cups per day to ease hot flashes and mood swings.

Caution: Avoid Sage in pregnancy. Red Clover is mildly estrogenic.

26. Cramp Relief (Muscle Spasm)

Ingredients:

- 1 tsp Motherwort
- 1 tsp Chamomile
- ½ tsp Ginger

Preparation: Infuse all herbs for 15 minutes. Add Ginger decoction.

Dosage: 1 cup every 6–8 hours during pain.

Caution: Avoid Motherwort during pregnancy.

27. Urinary Soothing Tea

Ingredients:

- 1 tsp Marshmallow Root
- 1 tsp Plantain Leaf
- ½ tsp Calendula

Preparation: Cold steep Marshmallow overnight. Steep other herbs and combine.

Dosage: 1 cup 2–3 times/day during symptoms.

Caution: None significant when prepared properly.

28. Digestive Bitters Tea (for sluggish digestion)

Ingredients:

- 1 tsp Dandelion Root
- 1 tsp Fennel
- ½ tsp Peppermint

Preparation: Simmer Dandelion; steep others separately and combine.

Dosage: ½–1 cup 20 minutes before meals.

Caution: Avoid Dandelion with gallstones or diuretics.

29. Heart + Nerve Harmony Tea

Ingredients:

- 1 tsp Hawthorn Leaf/Flower *(or substitute with Skullcap for calming)*
- 1 tsp Lemon Balm

- ½ tsp Motherwort

Preparation: Infuse herbs in hot water for 10–15 minutes.

Dosage: 1 cup 1–2x per day for mild heart palpitations and nervous tension.

Caution: Motherwort not for use in pregnancy.

30. Skin Glow Tea (From Within)

Ingredients:

- 1 tsp Calendula
- 1 tsp Red Clover
- ½ tsp Burdock Root

Preparation: Simmer Burdock, steep others. Mix and strain.

Dosage: 1 cup per day for 2–3 weeks.

Caution: Red Clover estrogenic; avoid if hormone-sensitive.

31. Eye Bright Tea (For Strained Eyes)

Ingredients:

- 1 tsp Chamomile
- 1 tsp Calendula
- ½ tsp Plantain

Preparation: Infuse in hot water, covered. Cool for warm compress use or drink.

Dosage: 1–2 cups daily or apply cooled tea topically.

Caution: Do not put directly in eyes unless sterile.

32. Gentle Detox Tea

Ingredients:

- 1 tsp Burdock Root
- 1 tsp Dandelion Leaf
- ½ tsp Red Clover

Preparation: Decoction of Burdock; infuse others and combine.

Dosage: 1 cup daily for 1–2 weeks.

Caution: Not for those on diuretics or hormone therapies.

33. Mood Lift Morning Tea

Ingredients:

- 1 tsp Holy Basil
- 1 tsp Lemon Balm
- ½ tsp Chamomile

Preparation: Steep in hot water for 10 minutes.

Dosage: 1 cup first thing in the morning.

Caution: None significant when taken at standard dose.

34. Pain Relief Anti-Spasm Tea

Ingredients:

- 1 tsp Skullcap
- 1 tsp Ginger
- ½ tsp Motherwort

Preparation: Simmer Ginger; steep others separately. Combine.

Dosage: 1 cup up to 3x per day as needed.

Caution: Avoid Motherwort in pregnancy; Ginger may thin blood.

35. Restorative Post-Illness Tea

Ingredients:

- 1 tsp Oatstraw
- 1 tsp Nettle
- ½ tsp Calendula

Preparation: Steep herbs together for 15–20 minutes.

Dosage: 1–2 cups per day during recovery phase.

Caution: None significant; gentle and restorative.

Chapter 8

Syrups & Decoctions

In the journey of herbal healing, **syrups and decoctions** stand as two of the most potent yet accessible methods of medicine-making. Where teas offer gentle nourishment and quiet rituals, syrups and decoctions dive deeper—pulling rich, grounding medicine from roots, barks, and seeds. They allow us to capture the full strength of an herb and preserve it in a form that's both powerful and palatable.

Syrups are sweet and soothing. They're especially beloved by children and elders. They're useful for **coughs, colds, immune support**, and any situation where you want your medicine to feel like a gift, not a chore.

Decoctions, in contrast, are earthy and deep. They're often bitter, strong, and deeply therapeutic. Used for **digestion, liver support, adrenal tonics, and respiratory ailments**, decoctions honor the parts of the plant that take time to offer up their healing essence.

This chapter will walk you through both methods in depth—how to make them, when to use them, what herbs suit them best, and what safety considerations you should be mindful of. Whether you're making a syrup for your child's sore throat or a decoction for your own fatigue, this knowledge will become part of your trusted herbal toolkit.

Making Herbal Syrups for Immunity

Herbal syrups are concentrated herbal infusions combined with a sweetener to enhance taste and preserve the remedy. They're ideal for treating children, soothing sore throats, easing coughs, and delivering strong herbal support in a form that feels comforting and familiar.

What Makes a Syrup Different?

- **Sweetened** for palatability and preservation
- **Thicker** than tea, but not as intense as tinctures
- **Soothing** to mucous membranes (especially with honey or Marshmallow Root)
- Can be used daily or at the first sign of illness

Tools Needed

- Stainless steel saucepan or enamel pot
- Fine mesh strainer or cheesecloth
- Measuring cups and spoons

- Sterile glass jars or bottles
- Funnel (optional, but helpful)

How to Make a Basic Syrup

An herbal syrup begins with a **decoction**, which is the slow simmering of tougher plant parts like roots, barks, seeds, or berries. This process draws out water-soluble medicinal compounds and prepares the base for a sweetened, shelf-stable remedy

Step 1: Make the Decoction

Use this whenever your recipe calls for a syrup base.

1. **Measure Your Herbs**

    - Use **1 oz of dried herb** (~3 tablespoons if chopped)
    - OR use **1 tablespoon of dried herb per 2 cups water** (for lighter applications)
    - If using fresh herbs, use 2–3 tablespoons per 2 cups water

2. **Simmer**

    - Combine herbs and cold water in a covered pot.
    - Bring to a gentle boil, then reduce to a simmer.
    - Simmer gently for **20–40 minutes**, or **until the liquid reduces by half** (you should end up with ~1 cup if starting with 2–3 cups of water).
    - The timing depends on herb toughness—roots and barks need closer to 40 minutes; flowers or leaves only 15–20 minutes.

3. **Strain Thoroughly**

    - Use cheesecloth or a fine mesh strainer.
    - Press the herbs firmly to extract all remaining liquid and nutrients.

At this point, you have a finished decoction, which you can use immediately as tea or store in the refrigerator for up to 48 hours for later use. But for syrup-making, continue with the steps below.

Step 2: Sweeten (Turning Decoction into Syrup)

1. **Choose Your Sweetener**

    - Add **½ to 1 cup of honey, molasses, or maple syrup** per cup of decoction liquid.
    - The more sweetener you add, the longer the shelf life.

2. **Incorporate Sweetener**

- Warm the strained decoction over **low heat** (do not boil, especially if using raw honey).
- Stir until fully dissolved and integrated.
- For added preservation, you may also include a splash of alcohol (see storage tips).

Step 3: Bottle and Store

1. **Bottle While Warm**

- Pour syrup into **sterilized glass jars or bottles** while still warm.
- Use a funnel to avoid spills.
- Label with herb name(s), ingredients, and date.

2. **Storage Options**

- **Refrigerator (standard):** Lasts **3–4 weeks** with honey or syrup
- **Extended (preserved):** Add **25% brandy or vodka by volume** for up to **3 months shelf life**

Typical Dosages

- **Adults**: 1 tablespoon, 2–3 times daily
- **Children**: 1 teaspoon, 2–3 times daily
- **Preventative**: 1 dose daily in cold/flu season

Notes Before You Begin

- Use **raw honey** for antimicrobial benefits (never for children under 1).
- **Vegetable glycerin** is a good alternative for alcohol-free, diabetic-friendly syrups.
- Strain well to avoid spoilage—any plant material left in can mold.

Using Roots & Barks in Decoctions

Decoctions are long-simmered herbal teas used to extract the medicine from **tougher plant parts**. While infusions work well for soft aerial parts like leaves and flowers, decoctions are required when you're working with **roots, bark, or hard seeds**.

They're earthy, grounding, and deeply medicinal. Their strength comes from time and fire.

Ideal Plants for Decoctions

- **Roots**: Burdock, Dandelion, Licorice, Elecampane, Ashwagandha
- **Barks**: Slippery Elm, Cinnamon
- **Seeds**: Fennel, Coriander
- **Tough stems**: Astragalus, Nettle root

How to Make a Decoction

1. **Measure**
   Use **1 oz of dried herb** (~3 tablespoons if chopped), or use **1 tablespoon of dried herb per 2 cups water** (for lighter applications)
2. If using fresh herbs, use 2–3 tablespoons per 2 cups water
3. **Simmer**
   Bring to a boil, reduce heat, and simmer gently **20–40 minutes** depending on the herb.
4. **Strain**
   Remove herbs and store in a clean jar.
5. **Use Immediately**
   Best fresh. Refrigerate unused portion and use within **48 hours**.

What Decoctions Are Best For:

- Chronic immune issues
- Deep-rooted fatigue
- Liver or adrenal support
- Digestive stimulation
- Lung cleansing

Decoction Tips

- Combine **roots** and **barks** in one pot, and **leaves or flowers** separately.
- For improved flavor and action, add aromatic herbs like **Ginger, Cinnamon, or Mint** in the final 5–10 minutes.

40 Syrup & Decoction Recipes

This chapter's heart lies in its rich recipe collection: **40 practical formulas** made entirely with Core 40 herbs. Each is designed to help you craft herbal solutions that are:

- Purposeful
- Affordable
- Safe
- Deeply effective

These recipes cover:

- Immunity & Cold Prevention
- Respiratory Support
- Digestion & Gut Health
- Mood & Nervous System
- Hormonal & Reproductive Wellness
- Liver, Skin & Inflammation
- Children's Health
- Post-illness Restoration

1. Elderberry Immune Syrup

Purpose: Preventative and acute immune support during cold/flu season

Ingredients:

- 1 cup dried Elderberries
- 1 tbsp Ginger (fresh or dried)
- 3 cups water
- 1 cup raw honey

Preparation:
Simmer Elderberries and Ginger in water for 30–40 minutes until reduced by half. Strain. Add honey and stir until well mixed. Bottle.

Dosage:
Adults: 1 Tbsp 2–3x/day
Children: 1 tsp 2x/day

Caution: Do not consume raw elderberries. Not for autoimmune conditions without guidance.

2. Throat Soothing Syrup

Purpose: Calms sore throat, cough, and voice strain

Ingredients:

- 2 tbsp Marshmallow Root
- 1 tbsp Licorice Root
- 2 cups water
- ¾ cup honey

Preparation:
Cold infuse Marshmallow overnight or simmer both herbs gently for 30 minutes. Strain and blend with honey.

Dosage:
Adults: 1 Tbsp every 2–4 hrs as needed
Children: 1 tsp

Caution: Avoid Licorice in hypertension or pregnancy without supervision.

3. Mullein Lung Decoction

Purpose: Helps dry, irritated lungs and coughing

Ingredients:

- 1 tbsp Mullein Leaf
- 1 tbsp Thyme
- 2 cups water

Preparation:
Simmer herbs 30 minutes. Strain through cloth to remove fuzz.

Dosage:
½–1 cup, up to 3x/day

Caution: Always strain Mullein thoroughly. Safe for children.

4. Yarrow Fever Brew

Purpose: Induces sweat, reduces fever, supports immunity

Ingredients:

- 1 tbsp Yarrow
- 1 tsp Peppermint
- 1 tsp Elderflower
- 2 cups water

Preparation:
Infuse in boiled water 15–20 min. Drink warm under a blanket.

Dosage:
1 cup every 2–4 hrs during fever

Caution: Not for people allergic to daisy family.

5. Licorice Root Cough Syrup

Purpose: Moistens and soothes dry, spasmodic cough

Ingredients:

- 1 tbsp Licorice Root
- 1 tsp Ginger
- 1½ cups water
- ¾ cup honey

Preparation:
Simmer herbs 30 minutes. Strain. Add honey and stir.

Dosage:
1 Tbsp every 3 hrs during cough

Caution: Avoid in hypertension, water retention, or pregnancy without guidance.

6. Echinacea Immunity Decoction

Purpose: Early-stage viral infections and immune stimulation

Ingredients:

- 1 tbsp Echinacea Root
- 1 tsp Ginger

- 2 cups water

Preparation:
Simmer for 25–30 minutes. Strain and serve warm.

Dosage:
½–1 cup every 4 hours for 3–5 days

Caution: Avoid long-term use or in autoimmune conditions.

7. Calendula Anti-Inflammatory Syrup

Purpose: Skin healing and lymphatic support (internal or topical)

Ingredients:

- 1 tbsp Calendula
- 1 tbsp Red Clover
- 2 cups water
- 1 cup honey

Preparation:
Infuse or simmer herbs for 20 min. Strain. Combine with honey.

Dosage:
1 Tbsp daily or as needed

Caution: Avoid if allergic to daisy family; Red Clover is mildly estrogenic.

8. Elecampane Respiratory Decoction

Purpose: Loosens deep lung congestion, helps wet cough

Ingredients:

- 1 tbsp Elecampane Root
- ½ tsp Ginger
- 2 cups water

Preparation:
Simmer 30 minutes. Strain and serve hot.

Dosage:
½–1 cup, 2–3x/day

Caution: Do not use in pregnancy. Strong flavor—blend with honey.

9. Thyme Honey Syrup

Purpose: Antibacterial, supports lungs, eases cough

Ingredients:

- 2 tbsp Thyme
- 1½ cups water
- ¾ cup raw honey

Preparation:
Infuse or simmer Thyme 20 minutes. Strain. Add honey while warm.

Dosage:
1 Tbsp up to 4x/day

Caution: Very safe. Avoid excess in pregnancy unless advised.

10. Nettle + Burdock Strengthening Decoction

Purpose: Mineral-rich tonic, supports kidneys, joints, and skin

Ingredients:

- 1 tbsp Nettle
- 1 tbsp Burdock Root
- 2½ cups water

Preparation:
Simmer 30–40 minutes. Strain and refrigerate up to 48 hours.

Dosage:
½–1 cup daily as tonic

Caution: Nettle is drying. Burdock may lower blood sugar—monitor if diabetic.

11. Fennel Digestive Syrup

Purpose: Eases bloating, gas, and mild cramping

Ingredients:

- 1 tbsp Fennel Seed
- 1 tsp Ginger
- 1½ cups water
- ¾ cup honey

Preparation:
Gently simmer Fennel and Ginger for 25 minutes. Strain and mix in honey.

Dosage:
1 Tbsp after meals

Caution: Avoid high doses during pregnancy.

12. Bitter Liver Decoction

Purpose: Supports sluggish digestion and bile production

Ingredients:

- 1 tbsp Dandelion Root
- 1 tbsp Burdock Root
- 2½ cups water

Preparation:
Simmer for 30–35 minutes. Strain and serve warm.

Dosage:
½ cup 15 minutes before meals

Caution: May act as a mild diuretic. Avoid if on lithium or diuretic drugs.

13. Nettle Mineral Syrup

Purpose: Builds strength, supports anemia and fatigue

Ingredients:

- 2 tbsp Nettle Leaf
- 1 tbsp Oatstraw
- 2½ cups water
- 1 cup molasses or honey

Preparation:
Simmer herbs 30 minutes. Strain and mix in sweetener.

Dosage:
1 Tbsp daily

Caution: Nettle may be too drying for some.

14. Lemon Balm Mood Syrup

Purpose: Calms nerves, uplifts mood, soothes tension

Ingredients:

- 2 tbsp Lemon Balm
- 1 tsp Lavender
- 2 cups water
- ¾ cup honey

Preparation:
Infuse herbs 15–20 minutes. Strain and blend with honey.

Dosage:
1–2 Tbsp during emotional stress

Caution: Avoid with hypothyroidism unless advised.

15. Holy Basil Adrenal Decoction

Purpose: Helps with stress fatigue, adrenal imbalance, foggy mind

Ingredients:

- 1 tbsp Holy Basil (Tulsi)
- 1 tsp Ginger
- 2½ cups water

Preparation:
Simmer herbs for 20 minutes. Strain.

Dosage:
½ to 1 cup morning and midday

Caution: Avoid during pregnancy.

16. Chamomile Tummy Syrup

Purpose: Great for nervous stomach, indigestion, or children's belly upset

Ingredients:

- 1½ tbsp Chamomile
- 1 tsp Fennel
- 1½ cups water
- ¾ cup honey

Preparation:
Steep herbs 15 minutes. Strain and add honey.

Dosage:
1 tsp for children; 1 Tbsp for adults

Caution: Allergy possible in those sensitive to daisies.

17. Skullcap Stress Decoction

Purpose: Calms overstimulation, racing thoughts, tension

Ingredients:

- 1 tbsp Skullcap
- 1 tsp Lemon Balm
- 2 cups water

Preparation:
Infuse or gently simmer 20 minutes. Strain.

Dosage:
1 cup before bed or during anxiety

Caution: Do not mix with other sedatives.

18. Licorice Root Energy Syrup

Purpose: Supports adrenal fatigue and low cortisol patterns

Ingredients:

- 1 tbsp Licorice Root
- 1 tsp Holy Basil
- 2 cups water
- ¾ cup honey

Preparation:
Simmer herbs 25–30 minutes. Strain and mix in honey.

Dosage:
1 Tbsp in morning only

Caution: Avoid in hypertension or during pregnancy.

19. Red Clover Cleansing Decoction

Purpose: Supports lymphatic flow, detoxification, and skin health

Ingredients:

- 1 tbsp Red Clover
- 1 tsp Burdock Root
- 2 cups water

Preparation:
Simmer gently 30 minutes. Strain and serve warm.

Dosage:
½ cup 1–2x/day

Caution: Avoid with estrogen-sensitive conditions.

20. Peppermint Clarity Syrup

Purpose: Refreshes focus, soothes tension headaches and brain fog

Ingredients:

- 1 tbsp Peppermint
- 1 tsp Rosemary
- 1½ cups water
- ¾ cup honey

Preparation:
Steep herbs for 15 minutes. Strain and add honey.

Dosage:
1 Tbsp during fatigue or headaches

Caution: Avoid Peppermint in reflux. Rosemary not advised in epilepsy or late pregnancy.

21. Raspberry Leaf Menstrual Tonic

Purpose: Tones the uterus, eases menstrual cramps, regulates cycles

Ingredients:

- 2 tbsp Raspberry Leaf
- 1 tsp Chamomile
- 2½ cups water

Preparation:
Infuse Raspberry and Chamomile in freshly boiled water for 20 minutes. Strain.

Dosage:
1 cup daily during the week before and during menstruation

Caution: Avoid in early pregnancy unless guided by a professional.

22. Motherwort Cramp Calmer

Purpose: Relieves tension, PMS irritability, and uterine spasms

Ingredients:

- 1 tbsp Motherwort
- 1 tsp Lemon Balm
- 2 cups water
- Optional: ½ tsp Ginger for circulation

Preparation:
Infuse all herbs in hot water for 15–20 minutes.

Dosage:
1 cup every 6 hours as needed during PMS or cramps

Caution: Avoid during pregnancy.

23. Red Clover Hormone Balancing Decoction

Purpose: Supports estrogen balance, fertility cleansing, and menopausal shifts

Ingredients:

- 1 tbsp Red Clover
- 1 tbsp Nettles
- 2½ cups water

Preparation:
Simmer for 25–30 minutes. Strain and drink warm.

Dosage:
1 cup daily for up to 3 weeks per cycle

Caution: Not recommended for estrogen-dominant conditions or if on hormonal meds.

24. Sage & Lavender Cooling Syrup

Purpose: Supports hot flashes, night sweats, and menopausal tension

Ingredients:

- 1 tbsp Sage
- 1 tsp Lavender
- 1½ cups water
- ¾ cup honey

Preparation:
Infuse herbs 20 minutes. Strain and combine with honey.

Dosage:
1 Tbsp morning and evening

Caution: Not for pregnant or breastfeeding women. May reduce milk supply.

25. Calendula Skin-Soothing Decoction

Purpose: Promotes clear skin, lymph flow, and wound healing

Ingredients:

- 1 tbsp Calendula
- 1 tbsp Burdock Root
- 2½ cups water

Preparation:
Simmer for 30 minutes. Strain. May also be applied topically on clean skin.

Dosage:
½ to 1 cup daily for 2 weeks

Caution: Avoid if allergic to daisy family. Discontinue if rash develops.

26. Burdock Root Liver Cleanse Brew

Purpose: Promotes detoxification, reduces hormonal acne and sluggish liver

Ingredients:

- 1 tbsp Burdock Root
- 1 tsp Dandelion Root
- 2½ cups water

Preparation:
Simmer roots for 30–40 minutes. Strain and drink warm.

Dosage:
1 cup daily for up to 3 weeks

Caution: Monitor blood sugar if diabetic.

27. Thyme + Sage Menstrual Cramp Syrup

Purpose: Combines antispasmodic and warming herbs for cramps and uterine tension

Ingredients:

- 1 tbsp Thyme
- 1 tbsp Sage
- 1½ cups water
- ¾ cup honey

Preparation:
Simmer for 20 minutes. Strain and blend with honey.

Dosage:
1 Tbsp every 6–8 hours during cramps

Caution: Avoid Sage during pregnancy or if breastfeeding.

28. Hibiscus Hormone Balancer

Purpose: Supports cardiovascular and reproductive balance, mildly cooling

Ingredients:

- 1 tbsp Hibiscus
- 1 tsp Lemon Balm
- 1 tsp Red Clover
- 2 cups water

Preparation:
Infuse in hot water for 15 minutes. Serve warm or iced.

Dosage:
1 cup up to 2x/day

Caution: Hibiscus may lower blood pressure; avoid Red Clover with hormonal therapy.

29. Marshmallow Root Urinary Relief Decoction

Purpose: Soothes urinary tract inflammation and irritation

Ingredients:

- 1½ tbsp Marshmallow Root
- 1 tsp Plantain Leaf (optional)
- 2½ cups water

Preparation:
Cold infusion overnight preferred. Strain before use.

Dosage:
1 cup 2–3 times/day during UTI or bladder discomfort

Caution: Extremely safe. Can delay absorption of medications—take herbs separately.

30. Skullcap Emotional Rescue Syrup

Purpose: Supports nervous system exhaustion, grief, and anxiety cycles

Ingredients:

- 1 tbsp Skullcap
- 1 tsp Lavender
- 1½ cups water
- ¾ cup honey

Preparation:
Steep Skullcap and Lavender 15–20 minutes. Combine with honey and bottle.

Dosage:
1 Tbsp as needed or before bed

Caution: Avoid with sedatives or alcohol. Not for use in pregnancy.

31. Oatstraw & Nettle Recovery Brew

Purpose: Deeply nourishing for fatigue, convalescence, burnout, or post-illness

Ingredients:

- 1 tbsp Oatstraw
- 1 tbsp Nettle
- 2½ cups water

Preparation:
Simmer 25–30 minutes. Strain and sip warm or cool.

Dosage:
1 cup daily for 2–3 weeks

Caution: Safe and well-tolerated. May be drying in some.

32. Children's Elderberry Syrup

Purpose: Gentle immune support for kids

Ingredients:

- ½ cup Elderberries
- 1 tsp Ginger
- 2 cups water
- ¾ cup raw honey

Preparation:
Simmer berries and ginger 30 minutes. Strain and cool before adding honey.

Dosage:
½ to 1 tsp twice daily (age 2+)

Caution: Do not give to infants under 1 due to honey. Never use raw elderberries.

33. Tulsi + Lemon Balm Nervous System Syrup

Purpose: Calms anxious minds, nourishes adrenals, and balances stress

Ingredients:

- 1 tbsp Holy Basil (Tulsi)
- 1 tbsp Lemon Balm
- 2 cups water
- ¾ cup honey

Preparation:
Infuse herbs 15–20 minutes. Strain and stir in honey.

Dosage:
1 Tbsp in morning and evening

Caution: Avoid Lemon Balm in hypothyroid conditions.

34. Digestion & Bloat Decoction

Purpose: Relieves post-meal heaviness, sluggish digestion, and gas

Ingredients:

- 1 tbsp Peppermint
- 1 tsp Fennel Seed
- ½ tsp Ginger
- 2 cups water

Preparation:
Simmer Ginger and Fennel. Add Peppermint at the end to steep. Strain.

Dosage:
½–1 cup after meals

Caution: Avoid Peppermint if you have acid reflux.

35. Elecampane Lung Recovery Brew

Purpose: For lingering cough, lung inflammation, and weakness

Ingredients:

- 1 tbsp Elecampane Root
- ½ tsp Licorice Root
- 2½ cups water

Preparation:
Simmer both herbs 30 minutes. Strain well.

Dosage:
½–1 cup twice daily for up to 7 days

Caution: Avoid during pregnancy.

36. Chamomile Night Syrup (For Kids)

Purpose: Calms restlessness, tummy tension, and sleep resistance

Ingredients:

- 1 tbsp Chamomile
- 1 tsp Lemon Balm
- 1½ cups water
- ½–¾ cup honey

Preparation:
Steep herbs for 10–15 minutes. Strain and add honey.

Dosage:
½ tsp for kids, 1 tsp for older children before bed

Caution: Test for daisy-family allergies first.

37. Immunity Builder Decoction (Daily Tonic)

Purpose: Strengthens immune reserves in cold season

Ingredients:

- 1 tbsp Astragalus Root
- 1 tbsp Echinacea Root
- 1 tsp Ginger
- 3 cups water

Preparation:
Simmer all for 40 minutes. Strain and store in fridge.

Dosage:
½ cup once or twice daily for prevention

Caution: Echinacea not for long-term use or autoimmune conditions.

38. Rosemary + Lemon Balm Clarity Syrup

Purpose: Enhances focus, memory, and uplifts mild melancholy

Ingredients:

- 1 tsp Rosemary
- 1 tbsp Lemon Balm
- 1½ cups water
- ¾ cup honey

Preparation:
Steep herbs in hot water for 20 minutes. Strain and mix with honey.

Dosage:
1 Tbsp mid-morning or early afternoon

Caution: Rosemary not advised for epilepsy or late pregnancy.

39. Calendula & Plantain Skin Recovery Tea

Purpose: Internal support for skin healing, wounds, and inflammation

Ingredients:

- 1 tbsp Calendula
- 1 tbsp Plantain Leaf
- 2½ cups water

Preparation:
Simmer gently for 25 minutes. Strain.

Dosage:
1 cup daily for 2–3 weeks

Caution: Avoid Calendula with daisy allergy.

40. Vital Roots Longevity Decoction

Purpose: Strengthening long-term tonic for energy, immunity, and resilience

Ingredients:

- 1 tbsp Ashwagandha (or substitute Burdock if preferred)
- 1 tbsp Dandelion Root
- 1 tsp Licorice Root
- 3 cups water

Preparation:
Simmer for 40 minutes. Strain and refrigerate.

Dosage:
½ cup daily for up to 6 weeks, then break

Caution: Avoid Licorice in hypertension; Ashwagandha in hyperthyroid states.

Chapter 9

Tinctures & Extracts

As your herbal journey deepens, you'll find yourself drawn to preparations that are both **powerful and portable**—this is where **tinctures** and **liquid extracts** shine.

Tinctures are **highly concentrated herbal remedies** preserved in alcohol, vinegar, or glycerin. With just a few drops under the tongue or in a glass of water, you can experience the essence of an herb—quickly, discreetly, and effectively. Unlike teas or syrups, tinctures require **no preparation at the time of use**, making them perfect for travel, emergencies, or daily tonic routines.

In this chapter, you'll learn the science and art of crafting your own tinctures. From choosing the right **solvent** to mastering **ratios and dosing**, this guide will ensure you extract herbs in a way that is **potent, shelf-stable, and safe**.

We'll then explore **40 tincture formulas** tailored to address common ailments—each using herbs from your **Core 40** collection. Whether you're crafting an immune elixir, a calming nervine blend, or a digestive bitters, tinctures offer serious medicine in a small, powerful bottle.

Solvents: Alcohol, Vinegar, Glycerin

Every tincture begins with two things: a **plant** and a **solvent**—the liquid that draws the medicine out. The choice of solvent affects not only what's extracted from the plant but also **how long it lasts**, **how it tastes**, and **who it's safe for**.

Let's break down your options:

Alcohol (Ethanol)

Why use it?
Alcohol is the **gold standard** for tincture-making. It extracts the **widest range of medicinal compounds**, including volatile oils, alkaloids, glycosides, and resins. It also preserves for years.

Best for:

- Roots, barks, resins, berries
- Emergency-use tinctures
- Long-term storage (5+ years)

Common types:

- Vodka (40% or 80 proof) for general use
- Grain alcohol (60–95%) for resinous or gummy herbs
- Brandy or rum for flavor and added energetics

Vinegar (Acetum)

Why use it?
Vinegar extracts **alkaloids and minerals** well and is a great choice for **nutritive herbs**. It's an excellent alcohol-free option and imparts a tangy flavor that blends well in dressings or tonics.

Best for:

- Nutritive herbs (Nettle, Red Clover, Dandelion leaf)
- Fresh herbs
- People avoiding alcohol (e.g., children, recovering alcoholics)

Shelf Life: 6–12 months

Glycerin (Glycerite)

Why use it?
Glycerin is **sweet, shelf-stable**, and gentle. It's ideal for **children**, animals, and sensitive individuals. It won't extract alkaloids or resins as well as alcohol but is excellent for **leaves and flowers**.

Best for:

- Nervines and relaxing herbs
- Children's blends
- Alcohol-free tinctures

Shelf Life: 6–12 months

Choosing the Right Solvent

Solvent	Best For	Shelf Life	Taste
Alcohol	Potent extractions	3–5+ years	Strong
Vinegar	Minerals, fresh greens	6–12 mo	Tart
Glycerin	Sensitive systems, kids	6–12 mo	Sweet

Herbal Ratios, Safety, and Dosing

One of the beauties of tincture-making is its **precision**. By using standardized ratios, you ensure consistency, safety, and repeatability.

Ratios

Tincture strength is based on **herb-to-solvent ratios** by weight (grams to milliliters):

- **Fresh herb tinctures**: 1:2
- **Dried herb tinctures**: 1:5

For example: 100g dried herb + 500ml alcohol = 1:5 tincture

Why it matters:

This allows herbalists to **standardize dosing**, especially when combining multiple herbs.

Alcohol Proof

- **40% (80 proof)**: Most leafy material
- **60–70%**: Standard for roots and barks
- **95% (190 proof)**: Used for resins, gums, and stubborn roots (or when making spagyrics)

Tincture-Making Steps

1. **Grind or chop** herbs
2. **Weigh** herbs and measure appropriate solvent
3. **Combine** in a glass jar with tight-fitting lid
4. **Shake daily** for 2–6 weeks
5. **Strain** through muslin or cheesecloth
6. **Bottle** in dark amber bottles with labels

General Dosing (Adults)

Purpose	Dosage
Acute illness	30–60 drops, 3–5x daily
Tonics	10–30 drops, 1–2x daily
Nervine support	15–25 drops before bed
Digestive bitters	5–15 drops 15 min before meals

20 drops ≈ 1 ml

Tincture Safety Guidelines

- **Always label**: Include herb name, date, ratio, and solvent type
- **Avoid contamination**: Use sterilized glass jars and clean utensils
- **Storage**: Keep in dark bottles, cool area, away from light
- **Herb-specific cautions**:
    - Licorice: not for high BP
    - Red Clover: avoid with estrogen therapies
    - Motherwort: contraindicated in pregnancy
    - Yarrow: allergy risk for daisy-sensitive individuals

40 Tincture Recipes by Ailment

The next section features **40 powerful tincture recipes**, tailored to address:

- Immunity & Cold Defense
- Digestive Health & Liver Support
- Nervous System & Sleep
- Hormonal Balance & Menstrual Health
- Inflammation & Pain
- Children's Health
- Long-Term Resilience

Immunity, Cold & Flu, Fever Support

1. Echinacea Root Immune Stimulator

Purpose: Supports immune function at the onset of illness

Ingredients:

- Dried Echinacea Root – 50g
- Alcohol (60–70%) – 250ml (1:5 ratio)

Preparation: Combine chopped root and alcohol in a jar. Shake daily for 4 weeks. Strain and bottle.

Dosage: 30–60 drops every 2–4 hrs at first sign of illness (max 7 days)

Caution: Avoid in autoimmune conditions or long-term use.

2. Elderberry Viral Defense

Purpose: Antiviral support, particularly for flu viruses

Ingredients:

- Dried Elderberries – 100g
- Vodka or Brandy (40%) – 200ml (1:2 fresh equivalent)

Preparation: Macerate for 4 weeks. Strain well and bottle.

Dosage: 1 dropper full (30 drops) 2–3x/day during outbreaks

Caution: Never use raw elderberries. Not for use in autoimmune flares.

3. Astragalus Daily Immune Tonic

Purpose: Builds immune resilience over time

Ingredients:

- Dried Astragalus Root – 50g
- Alcohol (60%) – 250ml (1:5)

Preparation: Chop root finely, macerate 4–6 weeks. Strain and bottle.

Dosage: 20–30 drops daily for 4–6 weeks

Caution: Not for use during acute fever. Use preventatively.

4. Thyme Lung & Infection Support

Purpose: Antibacterial, expectorant, supports wet or dry cough

Ingredients:

- Dried Thyme – 50g
- Alcohol (40%) – 250ml (1:5)

Preparation: Combine and steep for 2–4 weeks. Strain and store.

Dosage: 15–30 drops up to 4x/day for 7–10 days

Caution: High doses can be irritating to GI tract.

5. Yarrow Fever Aid

Purpose: Reduces fever and encourages perspiration

Ingredients:

- Dried Yarrow Flower – 25g
- Alcohol (40%) – 125ml (1:5)

Preparation: Macerate for 2–3 weeks. Strain, label, refrigerate if needed.

Dosage: 30 drops every 3 hours during fever

Caution: Avoid in pregnancy. May cause allergic reaction (daisy family).

6. Ginger Root Circulation Tincture

Purpose: Stimulates circulation, supports digestion, fights cold chills

Ingredients:

- Fresh Ginger Root – 100g
- Alcohol (50–60%) – 200ml (1:2 fresh)

Preparation: Chop fresh root. Steep in alcohol for 3–4 weeks. Strain.

Dosage: 10–20 drops before meals or during chills

Caution: Avoid in high fever or active ulcers.

7. Licorice Root Respiratory Rescue

Purpose: Soothes throat, supports adrenal fatigue, and helps cough

Ingredients:

- Dried Licorice Root – 50g
- Alcohol (60%) – 250ml (1:5)

Preparation: Steep for 4–6 weeks. Shake often. Strain and bottle.

Dosage: 10–30 drops up to 3x/day

Caution: Avoid with high blood pressure or pregnancy.

8. Mullein Lung Soother

Purpose: Eases dry, irritated lungs and cough

Ingredients:

- Dried Mullein Leaf – 50g
- Alcohol (40%) – 250ml (1:5)

Preparation: Strain through cloth to avoid fine hairs. Macerate 3 weeks.

Dosage: 20–40 drops up to 4x/day

Caution: Always strain Mullein thoroughly. Very safe herb.

9. Elecampane Deep Cough Relief

Purpose: Breaks up mucus, eases persistent cough

Ingredients:

- Dried Elecampane Root – 50g
- Alcohol (60–70%) – 250ml (1:5)

Preparation: Chop well. Steep for 4 weeks. Strain.

Dosage: 15–25 drops 2–3x/day

Caution: Avoid in pregnancy. May cause nausea in high doses.

10. Red Clover Gentle Immune Support

Purpose: Lymphatic support, blood purification

Ingredients:

- Dried Red Clover – 40g
- Alcohol (40%) – 200ml (1:5)

Preparation: Steep 3 weeks. Shake daily. Strain and store.

Dosage: 20–30 drops daily for long-term immune support

Caution: Avoid if using hormonal therapies or with estrogen dominance.

Digestion, Gut Healing, Liver & Gallbladder Support

11. Dandelion Root Liver Detox

Purpose: Stimulates bile flow, supports liver and digestion

Ingredients:

- Dried Dandelion Root – 50g
- Alcohol (60–70%) – 250ml (1:5)

Preparation:
Macerate 4–6 weeks. Strain and store in dark bottle.

Dosage:
15–30 drops 2–3x/day before meals

Caution:
Avoid with gallstones or bile duct obstruction.

12. Burdock Root Blood Cleanser

Purpose: Gently detoxifies, supports liver and skin clarity

Ingredients:

- Dried Burdock Root – 50g
- Alcohol (60%) – 250ml (1:5)

Preparation:
Chop and macerate 4 weeks. Strain and label.

Dosage:
15–30 drops 2x/day

Caution:
May lower blood sugar—monitor if diabetic.

13. Fennel Digestive Aid

Purpose: Reduces bloating, gas, and intestinal cramps

Ingredients:

- Dried Fennel Seed – 40g
- Alcohol (40%) – 200ml (1:5)

Preparation:
Macerate 2–3 weeks. Strain through fine cloth.

Dosage:
10–20 drops after meals

Caution:
Avoid in pregnancy in high doses.

14. Chamomile Calm Belly Tincture

Purpose: Relieves upset stomach, tension in gut, and indigestion

Ingredients:

- Dried Chamomile Flowers – 50g
- Alcohol (40%) – 250ml (1:5)

Preparation:
Infuse for 3 weeks. Shake daily. Strain well.

Dosage:
10–30 drops as needed, or before meals

Caution:
May cause reaction in those allergic to ragweed.

15. Ginger Root Warming Digestive

Purpose: Boosts sluggish digestion, eases nausea

Ingredients:

- Fresh Ginger Root – 100g
- Alcohol (60%) – 200ml (1:2 fresh)

Preparation:
Chop and macerate 3–4 weeks. Strain.

Dosage:
10–15 drops 15 min before meals

Caution:
Avoid in ulcers or during high fever.

16. Peppermint Stomach Soother

Purpose: Eases bloating, relieves spasms, clears gas

Ingredients:

- Dried Peppermint – 50g
- Alcohol (40%) – 250ml (1:5)

Preparation:
Macerate 2–3 weeks. Strain through cheesecloth.

Dosage:
10–20 drops after meals

Caution:
Avoid in reflux or hiatal hernia.

17. Calendula Gut Lining Repair

Purpose: Supports gut lining, leaky gut, and inflammation

Ingredients:

- Dried Calendula – 50g
- Alcohol (40%) – 250ml (1:5)

Preparation:
Infuse 3–4 weeks. Strain gently.

Dosage:
10–25 drops 2x/day

Caution:
Avoid with daisy allergies. Monitor for estrogenic effect.

18. Dandelion Leaf Digestive Bitter

Purpose: Increases bile and enzyme flow; useful for fatty digestion

Ingredients:

- Dried Dandelion Leaf – 50g
- Alcohol (40%) – 250ml (1:5)

Preparation:
Steep for 3 weeks. Strain and refrigerate if needed.

Dosage:
5–15 drops before meals

Caution:
Mild diuretic—monitor water intake.

19. Red Clover Gentle Detoxifier

Purpose: Promotes lymph flow, digestion, and elimination

Ingredients:

- Dried Red Clover – 50g
- Alcohol (40%) – 250ml (1:5)

Preparation:
Infuse 2–4 weeks. Strain and store in cool place.

Dosage:
10–30 drops daily

Caution:
Avoid if taking hormonal medications.

20. Licorice + Ginger Gut Harmonizer

Purpose: Soothes inflammation, repairs mucosa, supports adrenal/gut axis

Ingredients:

- Dried Licorice Root – 25g
- Fresh Ginger Root – 50g
- Alcohol (60%) – 250ml (blend)

Preparation:
Macerate 4 weeks. Shake daily. Strain and store.

Dosage:
10–20 drops before or after meals

Caution:
Avoid Licorice in high BP or pregnancy.

Hormonal Support, Menstrual Ease, Lymphatic Health

21. Raspberry Leaf Uterine Tonic

Purpose: Tones uterine muscles, supports menstrual health and fertility

Ingredients:

- Dried Raspberry Leaf – 50g

- Alcohol (40%) – 250ml (1:5)

Preparation:
Steep 2–4 weeks. Shake daily. Strain and bottle.

Dosage:
15–30 drops 1–2x/day before and during menstruation

Caution:
Avoid in early pregnancy unless guided.

22. Motherwort PMS Relief Blend

Purpose: Calms emotional PMS, eases uterine cramping and palpitations

Ingredients:

- Dried Motherwort – 50g
- Alcohol (40–50%) – 250ml (1:5)

Preparation:
Macerate for 4 weeks. Strain and store.

Dosage:
20–40 drops during PMS or cramping

Caution:
Avoid in pregnancy. May increase uterine tone.

23. Red Clover Hormonal Cleanser

Purpose: Supports lymphatic drainage and gentle hormone regulation

Ingredients:

- Dried Red Clover – 50g
- Alcohol (40%) – 250ml (1:5)

Preparation:
Steep 3 weeks. Strain and store in a cool place.

Dosage:
20–30 drops daily

Caution:
Avoid if on estrogen therapy or with hormone-sensitive conditions.

24. Lemon Balm Mood Support

Purpose: Relieves mild depression, emotional overwhelm, and tension

Ingredients:

- Dried Lemon Balm – 50g
- Alcohol (40%) – 250ml (1:5)

Preparation:
Macerate 2–3 weeks. Strain and refrigerate if needed.

Dosage:
10–20 drops up to 3x/day

Caution:
Avoid in hypothyroidism unless advised.

25. Hibiscus Hormonal Circulator

Purpose: Supports circulation, liver cleansing, and gentle cooling

Ingredients:

- Dried Hibiscus Flowers – 40g
- Alcohol (40%) – 200ml (1:5)

Preparation:
Macerate 2–4 weeks. Strain well through cloth.

Dosage:
20–30 drops up to 2x/day

Caution:
May lower blood pressure. Avoid in pregnancy unless advised.

26. Skullcap Menstrual Tension Relief

Purpose: Calms physical and emotional tension related to menstruation

Ingredients:

- Dried Skullcap – 50g
- Alcohol (40%) – 250ml (1:5)

Preparation:
Steep for 3 weeks. Shake daily. Strain.

Dosage:
15–25 drops at onset of discomfort or anxiety

Caution:
Not to be combined with sedatives or alcohol.

27. Calendula Lymph Cleanser

Purpose: Promotes lymphatic circulation and skin detoxification

Ingredients:

- Dried Calendula – 50g
- Alcohol (40%) – 250ml (1:5)

Preparation:
Macerate 3 weeks. Strain and bottle.

Dosage:
10–25 drops daily or during cleanse

Caution:
Avoid with daisy family allergies. Mild estrogenic effect.

28. Thyme Menstrual Support Tincture

Purpose: Relieves stagnation and cramping, promotes circulation

Ingredients:

- Dried Thyme – 40g
- Alcohol (40%) – 200ml (1:5)

Preparation:
Steep 2–3 weeks. Strain and store.

Dosage:
10–20 drops during menstrual discomfort

Caution:
May stimulate uterus; avoid high doses in pregnancy.

29. Burdock Hormonal Detoxifier

Purpose: Clears excess estrogen and supports skin/hormonal balance

Ingredients:

- Dried Burdock Root – 50g
- Alcohol (60%) – 250ml (1:5)

Preparation:
Chop and macerate 4 weeks. Strain and label.

Dosage:
15–30 drops daily for 3 weeks

Caution:
May lower blood sugar; monitor in diabetics.

30. Chamomile Emotional PMS Soother

Purpose: Reduces irritability, tension, and GI upset during PMS

Ingredients:

- Dried Chamomile – 50g
- Alcohol (40%) – 250ml (1:5)

Preparation:
Steep 3 weeks. Strain thoroughly to avoid sediment.

Dosage:
15–30 drops as needed

Caution:
Daisy allergy risk. May cause drowsiness in large amounts.

Children's Health, Recovery, Daily Tonic Support

31. Chamomile Children's Calm

Purpose: Soothes anxiety, teething, tummy troubles, and restlessness in children

Ingredients:

- Dried Chamomile – 40g
- Vegetable Glycerin – 200ml (1:5)

Preparation:
Glycerite method: steep herbs in 60% glycerin + 40% water for 3 weeks. Strain well.

Dosage:
5–10 drops for children, diluted in water or tea

Caution:
Always test for daisy-family allergy.

32. Lemon Balm Kid-Friendly Focus Aid

Purpose: Gently calms hyperactivity, improves attention and emotional regulation

Ingredients:

- Dried Lemon Balm – 40g
- Glycerin – 200ml (1:5)

Preparation:
Use glycerin or mild vinegar for extraction. Macerate 3 weeks. Strain.

Dosage:
5–15 drops 2x/day in water or juice

Caution:
Avoid in hypothyroid children.

33. Peppermint Tummy Tincture (Child-Safe)

Purpose: Eases bloating, colic, and digestive discomfort in little ones

Ingredients:

- Dried Peppermint – 30g
- Glycerin – 150ml (1:5)

Preparation:
Steep 2–3 weeks in glycerin. Strain through cloth.

Dosage:
5–10 drops after meals as needed

Caution:
Avoid if reflux is present.

34. Nettle Nourishing Mineral Tonic

Purpose: Strengthens bones, teeth, hair, and immunity in growing kids and adults

Ingredients:

- Dried Nettle Leaf – 50g
- Vinegar or Alcohol (40%) – 250ml (1:5)

Preparation:
Steep for 3–4 weeks. Strain. Use vinegar for calcium-rich blend.

Dosage:
10–20 drops daily with meals

Caution:
Can be drying; combine with moistening herbs like Licorice or Marshmallow.

35. Oatstraw Recovery + Nerve Support

Purpose: Rebuilds after illness, calms nervous system, nourishes depletion

Ingredients:

- Dried Oatstraw – 50g
- Alcohol (40%) – 250ml (1:5)

Preparation:
Steep 3 weeks. Shake daily. Strain well.

Dosage:
15–30 drops daily in water or tea

Caution:
Avoid if gluten-sensitive unless oat source is verified gluten-free.

36. Holy Basil (Tulsi) Daily Adaptogen

Purpose: Supports resilience, reduces stress, sharpens mind and breath

Ingredients:

- Dried Holy Basil – 50g
- Alcohol (40%) – 250ml (1:5)

Preparation:
Macerate 3–4 weeks. Strain thoroughly.

Dosage:
10–20 drops 2x/day

Caution:
Avoid during pregnancy or with blood-thinners.

37. Ashwagandha Energy & Sleep Balance

Purpose: Helps restore energy in fatigue while promoting restful sleep

Ingredients:

- Dried Ashwagandha Root – 50g
- Alcohol (60%) – 250ml (1:5)

Preparation:
Steep 4 weeks. Strain and label clearly.

Dosage:
15–30 drops 1x/day (evening preferred)

Caution:
Avoid with hyperthyroidism or in pregnancy.

38. Elecampane Lung Recovery Tincture

Purpose: Strengthens weak lungs after infection or asthma

Ingredients:

- Dried Elecampane – 50g
- Alcohol (60%) – 250ml (1:5)

Preparation:
Macerate 4–6 weeks. Strain and label clearly.

Dosage:
10–20 drops 2x/day

Caution:
Strong flavor. Blend with Licorice or Honey if needed.

39. Skullcap Gentle Nerve Rebuilder

Purpose: Supports post-burnout recovery, emotional fatigue, and trauma

Ingredients:

- Dried Skullcap – 50g
- Alcohol (40%) – 250ml (1:5)

Preparation:
Steep 3–4 weeks. Strain and store cool.

Dosage:
10–30 drops in evening or during stress

Caution:
Avoid mixing with sedatives or alcohol.

40. Adaptogen Resilience Blend

Purpose: Combines adaptogenic herbs for energy, immunity, and stress protection

Ingredients:

- Dried Holy Basil – 25g
- Ashwagandha Root – 25g
- Alcohol (50–60%) – 250ml total (1:5)

Preparation:
Blend herbs, macerate 4–6 weeks. Strain and store.

Dosage:
20–30 drops daily for 4–6 weeks

Caution:
Avoid in pregnancy or if using thyroid medications.

Chapter 10

Salves & Balms

Salves and balms are some of the **oldest and most trusted** herbal remedies. Unlike teas or tinctures that work internally, these preparations are applied directly to the **largest organ of your body—your skin.** They offer both **protection and nourishment**, making them essential for everyday scrapes, rashes, burns, dry skin, bruises, and even deeper discomforts like inflammation and nerve pain.

They're also deeply **hands-on and heart-centered** remedies. The act of applying a salve to a loved one, massaging a balm into sore hands, or crafting a jar for a friend transforms healing into a tangible act of care.

In this section, you'll learn:

- The **step-by-step method** for creating herbal oil infusions
- How to turn those oils into salves and balms with waxes and butters
- How to choose the **right herbs and base ingredients** for specific skin issues

And later, you'll find **40 beginner-safe salve and balm recipes** using the Core 40 herbs, to cover nearly every common skin or muscle issue.

Let's begin with the foundation: **oil infusion.**

Oil Infusion Techniques & Base Blending

To make a salve, you need to **first infuse a carrier oil** with the healing properties of your chosen herb. This infused oil becomes the "base" of your topical medicine.

1. Heat Infusion (Quick Method)

Best when you're short on time or working with **resins, roots, and tough herbs.**

Steps:

1. Fill a glass jar or double boiler with your **dried herb** (never fresh; water content causes spoilage).
2. Cover completely with a stable oil like **olive, sunflower,** or **coconut.**
3. Warm gently over **low heat (110–130°F)** for 2–4 hours. Do not fry or overheat.

4. Stir occasionally. Once the oil is richly colored and fragrant, strain through cheesecloth.
5. Store in a clean, dark jar away from sunlight.

2. Solar Infusion (Cold Method)

A slower but more **energetically gentle** method, especially for flowers and leafy herbs.

Steps:

1. Fill a glass jar halfway with dried herb.
2. Pour oil over the herbs until the jar is nearly full.
3. Seal tightly and place on a sunny windowsill for **3–6 weeks**, shaking gently every day.
4. After infusion, strain thoroughly with cheesecloth or a fine strainer.
5. Store the infused oil in a dark glass bottle, labeled with the herb name and date.

Choosing Your Oil Base

Different oils offer different benefits. Pick based on your skin type, herbal use, and shelf life.

Oil	Skin Type	Benefits
Olive Oil	All skin types	Stable, healing, affordable, resists oxidation
Coconut Oil	Hot, inflamed skin	Cooling, antimicrobial, hardens when cool
Jojoba Oil	Oily, acne-prone	Mimics sebum, absorbs fast, long shelf life
Sunflower Oil	Sensitive or baby skin	Lightweight, gentle, fast absorbing
Almond Oil	Dry, irritated skin	Soothing, mild scent, pairs well with flowers
Grapeseed Oil	Normal to oily skin	Light, tightens skin, shorter shelf life

Pro tip: Combine 2–3 oils to balance moisturizing and healing properties.

Turning Infused Oils into Salves & Balms

To give your infused oil body and structure, you'll add a **hardener**—usually **beeswax**—and optionally **butters** or **essential oils**.

What's the Difference?

Type	Texture	Use Case
Salve	Soft, ointment-like	Great for large areas, easy to apply
Balm	Firmer, waxier	Ideal for lips, solid perfumes, spot use

Basic Salve Recipe (Foundation for All Others)

Ingredients:

- 1 cup infused oil
- 1 oz beeswax (adjust for firmness)
- Optional: 10–15 drops essential oil (e.g., lavender, tea tree)

Steps:

1. Heat oil and beeswax in a **double boiler** until fully melted.
2. Remove from heat. Stir in essential oils, if using.
3. Quickly pour into tins or jars.
4. Let cool uncovered. Cap and label.

Basic Balm Recipe (Firmer Texture)

Ingredients:

- **1 cup infused oil** *(e.g., Calendula, Plantain, Lavender)*
- **1.5 oz beeswax** *(for a firmer consistency)*
- **Optional**: 10–15 drops essential oil *(Lavender for calming, Peppermint for cooling, Tea Tree for antibacterial)*

Steps:

1. In a **double boiler**, gently melt the beeswax into the infused oil over low heat.
2. Once fully melted, remove from heat.
3. Add essential oils (if using) and stir well to distribute evenly.
4. Immediately pour into **lip balm tubes, small tins, or glass jars**.
5. Allow to cool and harden completely, uncovered.
6. Cap and **label clearly** with date, herbs, and intended use.

Tips for Adjustments:

- For an **ultra-firm balm** (like solid perfume or foot balm), use **2 oz beeswax per cup of oil**.
- Add a small amount of **cocoa or shea butter** for additional skin nourishment and aroma.
- If the balm is too firm once cooled, remelt and add a little more oil.

Healing Formulas for Skin, Pain & Inflammation

Your choice of **herbs and bases** determines what your salve or balm will treat. Below are categories to guide your herbal choices.

1. Wound Healing & Regeneration

Use For: Cuts, scrapes, surgical scars, abrasions

Best Herbs:

- **Calendula**: Antibacterial, anti-inflammatory, speeds tissue repair
- **Yarrow**: Stops bleeding, prevents infection
- **Plantain**: Pulls out debris, soothes itch and pain
- **Comfrey**: Speeds healing of shallow, non-infected wounds

2. Pain & Inflammation Relief

Use For: Muscle soreness, bruises, sprains, nerve pain, arthritis

Best Herbs:

- **St. John's Wort**: Nerve pain and inflammation
- **Arnica**: Bruises and trauma (only on unbroken skin)
- **Ginger**: Warms, increases circulation
- **Cayenne**: Stimulates blood flow, relieves joint stiffness

Base Oils: Combine coconut and olive for a warming effect

Caution: Test warming herbs like cayenne on a small patch first!

3. Soothing Rashes & Irritated Skin

Use For: Eczema, diaper rash, sensitive skin, insect bites

Best Herbs:

- **Chamomile**: Gentle anti-inflammatory, calming
- **Marshmallow**: Moisturizing and soothing
- **Lavender**: Antibacterial and calming
- **Chickweed**: Draws out heat and itch

Recommended Base: Sunflower or jojoba for mild skin

4. Antibacterial & Antifungal Use

Use For: Acne, athlete's foot, minor infections, ringworm

Best Herbs:

- **Thyme**: Antimicrobial powerhouse
- **Tea Tree Oil** *(essential oil only)*: Potent antifungal
- **Calendula**: Prevents infection, heals minor wounds

Tip: Use coconut oil for its added antibacterial benefits.

5. Protective & Moisturizing Balms

Use For: Dry lips, windburn, cracked heels, harsh weather

Best Bases:

- **Shea Butter**: Deeply hydrating, rich in fatty acids
- **Cocoa Butter**: Protects and softens
- **Beeswax**: Locks in moisture

Optional Additions:

- Vitamin E oil (preservative + skin repair)
- Lavender essential oil (gentle scent + skin support)

In the next section, you'll find **45 beginner-friendly recipes** for salves and balms using the **Core 40 herbs**. Each formula has been crafted for a specific use—from bug bites and burns to nerve pain and diaper rash.

45 Salve & Balm Recipes

Wound Care, First Aid, and Skin Regeneration

1. Calendula Healing Salve (Salve)

Base Oil: Calendula-infused olive oil
Use: Wound healing, cuts, minor burns
Directions: Apply 2–3x/day to clean skin for healing.

Ingredients:

- 1 cup Calendula-infused oil
- 1 oz beeswax
- Optional: 5–10 drops lavender essential oil

Instructions:

1. Warm oil and beeswax in a double boiler until melted.
2. Remove from heat and stir in essential oil.
3. Pour into sterilized tins or jars.
4. Cool uncovered. Cap and label.

Caution: Avoid use if allergic to plants in the Asteraceae (daisy) family. Not for deep or infected wounds.

2. Plantain Drawing Balm (Balm)

Base Oil: Plantain-infused sunflower oil
Use: Splinters, stings, minor infections
Directions: Apply and cover with bandage; reapply as needed.

Ingredients:

- 1 cup Plantain-infused oil
- 1.5 oz beeswax
- Optional: ½ tsp activated charcoal

Instructions: Same as above.

Caution: For external use only. Do not apply to deep or puncture wounds without supervision.

3. Yarrow Quick-Stop Salve (Salve)

Base Oil: Yarrow-infused oil
Use: Bleeding wounds, fresh cuts
Directions: Dab lightly on bleeding areas (avoid deep wounds).

Ingredients:

- 1 cup Yarrow-infused oil
- 1 oz beeswax

Instructions: Prepare as in standard salve method.

Caution: Avoid in those with allergies to yarrow or other members of the daisy family. Not for deep or heavily soiled wounds.

4. Comfrey Skin-Knit Balm (Balm)

Base Oil: Comfrey-infused oil
Use: Bruises, cracked skin, scar support
Directions: Massage gently on bruised or cracked skin (not on open wounds).

Ingredients:

- 1 cup Comfrey-infused oil
- 1.5 oz beeswax
- Optional: 1 tsp vitamin E oil

Instructions: Use standard balm method.

Caution: Do not apply to open wounds. Comfrey speeds skin healing but may trap infection inside if the wound is not fully clean.

5. Chamomile Rash Relief Salve (Salve)

Base Oil: Chamomile-infused oil
Use: Eczema, baby rashes, skin irritations
Directions: Apply thin layer to inflamed areas 2x/day.

Ingredients:

- 1 cup Chamomile-infused oil
- 1 oz beeswax

Instructions: Prepare using standard salve process.

Caution: Chamomile is in the daisy family. Patch test before use if allergies are suspected.

6. Lavender Soothing Balm (Balm)

Base Oil: Lavender-infused jojoba oil
Use: Burns, sunburn, tension balm
Directions: Apply sparingly to affected area. Safe for lips and face.

Ingredients:

- 1 cup Lavender-infused oil
- 1.5 oz beeswax
- Optional: 10 drops lavender essential oil

Instructions: Use balm preparation method.

Caution: Avoid contact with eyes. While generally safe, test a small area first for sensitive skin reactions.

7. Calendula + Plantain Rescue Salve (Salve)

Base Oil: Blend of calendula + plantain-infused oils
Use: Scrapes, scratches, surface wounds
Directions: Apply liberally after cleansing skin.

Ingredients:

- ½ cup Calendula-infused oil

- ½ cup Plantain-infused oil
- 1 oz beeswax

Instructions: Follow salve process, blend oils before melting.

Caution: Do not use on infected or weeping wounds without supervision. Calendula may cause irritation in people allergic to daisies.

8. Nettle Anti-Itch Balm (Balm)

Base Oil: Nettle-infused oil
Use: Hives, allergic rashes, itching
Directions: Rub gently as needed, especially after exposure.

Ingredients:

- 1 cup Nettle-infused oil
- 1.5 oz beeswax

Instructions: Prepare using balm method.

Caution: Nettle can be slightly drying. If irritation occurs, combine with a more moistening oil like marshmallow or reduce use.

9. Chickweed Cooling Salve (Salve)

Base Oil: Chickweed-infused sunflower oil
Use: Hot rashes, bug bites, prickly heat
Directions: Use on itchy or irritated skin as needed.

Ingredients:

- 1 cup Chickweed-infused oil
- 1 oz beeswax
- Optional: 5 drops peppermint essential oil

Instructions: Melt and combine oils and beeswax, pour and cool.

Caution: Peppermint essential oil may be too strong for infants or broken skin—omit for sensitive users.

10. Yarrow + Lavender Healing Balm (Balm)

Base Oil: Blend of yarrow and lavender oils
Use: Scabs, scar support, post-suture skin recovery
Directions: Apply twice daily to clean skin.

Ingredients:

- ½ cup Yarrow-infused oil
- ½ cup Lavender-infused oil
- 1.5 oz beeswax

Instructions: Prepare as balm, blend oils before heating.

Caution: Do not use near eyes. Yarrow may cause skin irritation in those sensitive to daisy-family plants.

Pain, Bruises, Inflammation & Joint Support

11. Arnica Muscle Recovery Balm (Balm)

Base Oil: Arnica-infused olive oil
Use: Sore muscles, bruises, post-workout relief
Directions: Rub onto unbroken skin after physical activity or strain.

Ingredients:

- 1 cup Arnica-infused oil
- 1.5 oz beeswax
- Optional: 5 drops peppermint or eucalyptus essential oil

Caution: Do not use on broken skin. Avoid during pregnancy and in those allergic to the daisy family.

12. St. John's Wort Nerve Pain Salve (Salve)

Base Oil: St. John's Wort-infused olive or sunflower oil
Use: Sciatica, neuralgia, nerve pain, sunburn
Directions: Apply 2x/day along the affected nerve area.

Ingredients:

- 1 cup St. John's Wort-infused oil
- 1 oz beeswax

Caution: External use only. May increase sensitivity to sunlight (photosensitizing). Avoid during pregnancy.

13. Ginger Warming Joint Balm (Balm)

Base Oil: Ginger-infused sesame or olive oil
Use: Cold, stiff joints, arthritis, poor circulation
Directions: Massage into joints and cover for warmth.

Ingredients:

- 1 cup Ginger root-infused oil
- 1.5 oz beeswax
- Optional: 5 drops cinnamon essential oil

Caution: Avoid on broken or inflamed skin. Patch test to avoid burning sensations.

14. Cayenne Circulation Balm (Balm)

Base Oil: Cayenne-infused olive oil
Use: Stimulates blood flow, eases chronic cold hands/feet, arthritis
Directions: Massage into affected areas sparingly.

Ingredients:

- 1 cup Cayenne-infused oil
- 1.5 oz beeswax

Caution: May cause a warming or burning sensation. **Avoid eyes, mucous membranes, and open wounds.** Always wash hands after use.

15. Turmeric Inflammation Salve (Salve)

Base Oil: Turmeric-infused coconut or olive oil
Use: Joint pain, swelling, inflammatory skin issues
Directions: Rub gently into inflamed areas 2x/day.

Ingredients:

- 1 cup Turmeric-infused oil
- 1 oz beeswax

Caution: May stain skin and fabrics. Avoid on open wounds. Patch test for yellowing.

16. Comfrey + Arnica Joint Balm (Balm)

Base Oil: Blend of Comfrey and Arnica oils
Use: Bruised, sore joints, old injuries
Directions: Massage firmly into muscles or joints 2–3x/day.

Ingredients:

- ½ cup Comfrey oil
- ½ cup Arnica oil
- 1.5 oz beeswax

Caution: Not for open wounds. Avoid in pregnancy and with daisy allergies.

17. Peppermint Cooling Pain Balm (Balm)

Base Oil: Peppermint-infused olive oil
Use: Headaches (temples), sore muscles, cooling effect
Directions: Apply to neck, temples, or sore areas sparingly.

Ingredients:

- 1 cup Peppermint-infused oil
- 1.5 oz beeswax
- Optional: 5 drops peppermint essential oil

Caution: Do not apply near eyes or broken skin. May be too cooling for young children.

18. Lavender Anti-Spasm Salve (Salve)

Base Oil: Lavender-infused oil
Use: Muscle spasms, tension, menstrual cramps
Directions: Apply to abdomen, shoulders, or tense areas.

Ingredients:

- 1 cup Lavender-infused oil
- 1 oz beeswax

Caution: Patch test for sensitive skin. Lavender is gentle but potent—avoid in low blood pressure.

19. Holy Basil (Tulsi) Tension Balm (Balm)

Base Oil: Holy Basil-infused oil
Use: Headaches, shoulder tightness, mental fatigue
Directions: Massage onto temples, chest, or neck.

Ingredients:

- 1 cup Tulsi-infused oil
- 1.5 oz beeswax

Caution: Avoid contact with eyes. Strong aromatic herbs—test small area before wide use.

20. Calendula + St. John's Wort Nerve Salve (Salve)

Base Oil: Half Calendula, half St. John's Wort
Use: Nerve damage, post-shingles, neuralgia
Directions: Massage gently into affected area twice daily.

Ingredients:

- ½ cup Calendula oil
- ½ cup St. John's Wort oil
- 1 oz beeswax

Caution: Sun sensitivity is possible. Not for use on deep wounds. Monitor for allergic response.

Skin Soothing, Rash Relief, and Gentle Balms for Babies

21. Chamomile Eczema Soothing Salve (Salve)

Base Oil: Chamomile-infused sunflower oil
Use: Eczema, dry patches, redness, irritation
Directions: Apply thin layer 2–3x daily to affected skin.

Ingredients:

- 1 cup Chamomile-infused oil
- 1 oz beeswax

Caution: Patch test for allergies (daisy family). Avoid contact with eyes.

22. Chickweed Itch Relief Balm (Balm)

Base Oil: Chickweed-infused olive oil
Use: Itching from eczema, hives, bug bites
Directions: Apply as needed to itchy or hot skin.

Ingredients:

- 1 cup Chickweed-infused oil
- 1.5 oz beeswax
- Optional: 3 drops peppermint essential oil (omit for kids)

Caution: Peppermint may be too strong for young children or sensitive skin. Avoid open wounds.

23. Calendula Baby Bottom Balm (Balm)

Base Oil: Calendula-infused olive or sunflower oil
Use: Diaper rash, skin folds, baby irritations
Directions: Apply with clean hands during diaper changes.

Ingredients:

- 1 cup Calendula-infused oil
- 1.5 oz beeswax
- Optional: 1 tsp zinc oxide (barrier)

Caution: Gentle and safe, but do not use on open wounds or infected rashes without supervision.

24. Lavender Bedtime Balm (Balm)

Base Oil: Lavender-infused jojoba oil
Use: Calms restlessness, supports bedtime rituals
Directions: Rub on chest, feet, or temples before sleep.

Ingredients:

- 1 cup Lavender-infused oil
- 1.5 oz beeswax
- Optional: 4–6 drops lavender essential oil

Caution: Safe for most children, but avoid near eyes or mouth.

25. Marshmallow Moisture Salve (Salve)

Base Oil: Marshmallow root-infused oil
Use: Dry, cracked, peeling skin, windburn
Directions: Apply generously after bathing or exposure.

Ingredients:

- 1 cup Marshmallow-infused oil
- 1 oz beeswax

Caution: Safe for all ages. Avoid contamination; use clean fingers or spoon.

26. Lemon Balm Gentle Face Balm (Balm)

Base Oil: Lemon Balm-infused oil (glycerin-prepped if needed)
Use: Redness, sensitive face skin, mild cold sores
Directions: Apply to clean skin 1–2x/day.

Ingredients:

- 1 cup Lemon Balm-infused oil
- 1.5 oz beeswax

Caution: May irritate very sensitive skin. Avoid in hypothyroidism.

27. Lavender + Chamomile Baby Calm Balm (Balm)

Base Oil: ½ Lavender, ½ Chamomile-infused oil
Use: Cradle cap, mild skin irritations, bedtime rub
Directions: Massage gently onto baby's scalp or chest.

Ingredients:

- 1 cup blended oil
- 1.5 oz beeswax

Caution: Always patch test for sensitive infants. Avoid near eyes or nose.

28. Calendula + Chickweed Rash Salve (Salve)

Base Oil: ½ Calendula, ½ Chickweed-infused oil
Use: Rashes, eczema, post-shave irritation
Directions: Use 2–3x/day on clean, dry skin.

Ingredients:

- 1 cup blended oil
- 1 oz beeswax

Caution: Check for daisy-family allergies. Store in cool place.

29. Lavender & Marshmallow Lip Balm (Balm)

Base Oil: ½ Lavender, ½ Marshmallow-infused oil
Use: Chapped lips, cracked corners, windburn
Directions: Apply as needed throughout the day.

Ingredients:

- 1 cup blended oil
- 1.5 oz beeswax
- Optional: 1 tsp honey (natural humectant)

Caution: Omit honey for infants under 1 year.

30. Nettle Nourishing Skin Balm (Balm)

Base Oil: Nettle-infused olive or sunflower oil
Use: Nutrient-rich skin support for dry, aging skin
Directions: Apply to face or hands daily.

Ingredients:

- 1 cup Nettle-infused oil
- 1.5 oz beeswax

Caution: Can be slightly drying—combine with marshmallow or calendula if needed for balance.

Protective, Antifungal, Lip & Everyday Use

31. Thyme Antifungal Balm (Balm)

Base Oil: Thyme-infused olive oil
Use: Athlete's foot, toenail fungus, ringworm
Directions: Apply 2x/day to clean, dry skin.

Ingredients:

- 1 cup Thyme-infused oil
- 1.5 oz beeswax
- Optional: 3–5 drops tea tree essential oil

Caution: Avoid contact with eyes or mucous membranes. Patch test for sensitive skin.

32. Calendula Protective Skin Shield (Balm)

Base Oil: Calendula-infused oil
Use: Barrier balm for dry, cracked, weather-exposed skin
Directions: Rub into hands, lips, or face before cold/windy weather.

Ingredients:

- 1 cup Calendula oil
- 1.5 oz beeswax
- Optional: 1 tsp cocoa butter

Caution: Safe and gentle. Avoid overuse on oily skin types.

33. Lavender Cold Sore Relief Balm (Balm)

Base Oil: Lavender-infused jojoba oil
Use: Helps soothe and dry cold sores in early stage
Directions: Dab gently 3–4x/day at onset.

Ingredients:

- 1 cup Lavender oil
- 1.5 oz beeswax
- Optional: 5 drops lemon balm essential oil

Caution: Avoid sharing container. Not for open wounds.

34. Nettle & Marshmallow Dry Skin Rescue (Balm)

Base Oil: ½ Nettle, ½ Marshmallow-infused oil
Use: Rough elbows, heels, knees
Directions: Rub generously after showering or before bed.

Ingredients:

- 1 cup total blended oil
- 1.5 oz beeswax

Caution: Store in cool area. Patch test for balance (nettles can be drying).

35. Lemon Balm Lip Defense Balm (Balm)

Base Oil: Lemon Balm-infused oil
Use: Cold sore prevention, lip hydration, herbal gloss
Directions: Apply morning and night or as needed.

Ingredients:

- 1 cup Lemon Balm oil
- 1.5 oz beeswax
- Optional: 1 tsp honey (humectant)

Caution: Avoid in known thyroid disorders unless advised.

36. Red Clover Skin Detox Salve (Salve)

Base Oil: Red Clover-infused oil
Use: Skin purification, acne-prone areas, lymphatic congestion
Directions: Apply thinly on areas of congestion or skin imbalance.

Ingredients:

- 1 cup Red Clover oil
- 1 oz beeswax

Caution: Avoid with hormone-sensitive conditions.

37. Arnica + Peppermint Bruise Balm (Balm)

Base Oil: Arnica-infused oil
Use: Bruises, muscle knocks, sore limbs
Directions: Massage gently into bruised area 2–3x/day.

Ingredients:

- 1 cup Arnica oil
- 1.5 oz beeswax
- Optional: 5 drops peppermint oil

Caution: Not for broken skin. Avoid during pregnancy and with daisy allergies.

38. Holy Basil Stress Relief Balm (Balm)

Base Oil: Tulsi-infused oil
Use: Calms tension, supports mindfulness, great for temples and wrists
Directions: Apply to pulse points or rub into chest.

Ingredients:

- 1 cup Holy Basil oil
- 1.5 oz beeswax

Caution: May interact with blood sugar levels; avoid during pregnancy.

39. Marshmallow Lip Softening Balm (Balm)

Base Oil: Marshmallow-infused oil
Use: Dry lips, windburned cheeks, kids' winter care
Directions: Apply as needed throughout day.

Ingredients:

- 1 cup Marshmallow oil
- 1.5 oz beeswax
- Optional: 1 tsp cocoa butter

Caution: Safe for children. Avoid double-dipping—use clean fingers.

40. Ginger Circulation Balm (Balm)

Base Oil: Ginger-infused sesame oil
Use: Cold hands and feet, arthritis, low circulation
Directions: Rub on affected area and cover for warmth.

Ingredients:

- 1 cup Ginger oil
- 1.5 oz beeswax

Caution: Avoid mucous membranes. Slight burning may occur—patch test first.

41. Calendula + Lavender Skin Recovery Balm (Balm)

Base Oil: Equal blend of Calendula + Lavender-infused oil
Use: Post-injury or surgery scar softening, rash support
Directions: Apply to skin twice daily after scab formation.

Ingredients:

- 1 cup total oil
- 1.5 oz beeswax

Caution: Avoid in case of daisy-family allergies.

42. Thyme + Lavender Acne Spot Balm (Balm)

Base Oil: Thyme + Lavender-infused oil
Use: Spot treatment for inflamed pimples or acne outbreaks
Directions: Dab directly onto blemish 2x/day.

Ingredients:

- 1 cup oil
- 1.5 oz beeswax

Caution: May be drying—avoid overuse on sensitive skin.

43. Chamomile Baby Cheek Balm (Balm)

Base Oil: Chamomile-infused oil
Use: Red cheeks, windburn, mild drool rash
Directions: Apply sparingly with clean hands.

Ingredients:

- 1 cup oil
- 1.5 oz beeswax

Caution: Safe for babies. Test first near jawline before full use.

44. Calendula + Nettle Gardener's Hand Balm (Balm)

Base Oil: Half Calendula, Half Nettle
Use: Calloused hands, dry cracked fingers, post-gardening care
Directions: Rub into hands at night, wear gloves for deep treatment.

Ingredients:

- 1 cup total oil
- 1.5 oz beeswax

Caution: Store cool. Safe for daily use.

45. All-Purpose Herbal First Aid Balm (Balm)

Base Oil: Blend of Calendula, Plantain, Yarrow
Use: Cuts, stings, cracked skin, minor burns, rash
Directions: Apply thin layer to clean, dry skin as needed.

Ingredients:

- ⅓ cup each infused oil
- 1.5 oz beeswax
- Optional: 5 drops lavender essential oil

Caution: Do not apply to puncture wounds. Check for Asteraceae family allergies.

Chapter 11

Herbal Kitchen: Seasonings, Butters & More

Herbal medicine doesn't just belong in a tincture bottle or a balm tin—it belongs at the center of your kitchen. The foods we eat every day are opportunities to nourish our bodies with herbs that heal, protect, and invigorate.

Chapter 11 is all about infusing your culinary life with herbal medicine. These recipes are not only flavorful but functional. They allow you to incorporate the Core 40 herbs into sauces, seasonings, butters, oils, vinegars, and even nourishing treats that promote wellness while satisfying the senses.

This chapter is divided into two sections:

1. **Foundational Techniques** – How to make herbal vinegars, salts, and butters using from among the Core 40 herbs.

2. **50 Herbal Kitchen Recipes** – Practical and delicious applications of those techniques for everyday meals and healing rituals.

Whether you're new to herbal kitchen crafting or looking to expand your repertoire, this chapter brings plants off the shelf and into the heart of the home: your plate.

Making Herbal Vinegars, Salts, & Butters

Herbal Vinegars

Herbal vinegars are tangy, versatile infusions that preserve the medicinal qualities of plants in a delicious medium. They support digestion, balance blood sugar, and extract minerals like calcium and magnesium from leafy herbs.

Great Herbs for Vinegars:

- Nettle (mineral-rich)
- Red Clover (lymphatic support)
- Basil (antioxidant, flavorful)
- Garlic (antimicrobial)
- Thyme (immune and respiratory support)

1. Nettle Mineral Vinegar

Purpose: Builds iron, calcium, and vital trace minerals
Ingredients:

- 1 cup dried nettle
- 2 cups raw apple cider vinegar

Instructions:

1. Fill a quart jar halfway with dried nettle.
2. Cover completely with vinegar and seal with a non-metal lid.
3. Steep 3–4 weeks in a dark place.
4. Strain and store in glass bottle.

Use: Add 1–2 tbsp to warm water before meals or use in salad dressings.
Caution: Avoid if you're on diuretics or have kidney issues without practitioner guidance.

2. Red Clover Vinegar Tonic

Purpose: Supports hormonal balance and lymphatic flow
Ingredients:

- 1 cup red clover blossoms
- 2 cups apple cider vinegar

Instructions:
Steep and strain like other vinegars. Keep in dark place.

Use: Add to green salads or seltzer water with a splash of honey.
Caution: Not advised for estrogen-sensitive conditions.

3. Garlic & Thyme Fire Cider

Purpose: Immune support, clears sinus & congestion
Ingredients:

- ½ cup chopped garlic
- ¼ cup fresh thyme (or 2 tbsp dried)
- 2 tbsp grated horseradish
- 1 tbsp black peppercorns

- Apple cider vinegar to cover

Instructions:

1. Place herbs in a mason jar, cover with vinegar.
2. Let steep 2–4 weeks.
3. Strain and store in a dark bottle. Add honey to taste (optional).

Use: 1 tbsp daily as immune tonic, or more when sick.
Caution: Spicy! May irritate ulcers or GERD.

Herbal Salts

Herbal salts are one of the easiest ways to use herbs daily. By combining dried herbs with mineral-rich sea salt or Himalayan salt, you create a flavorful, healing addition to every meal.

Popular Herb Choices:

- Rosemary (stimulating and circulatory)
- Sage (warming and anti-inflammatory)
- Oregano (antimicrobial)
- Thyme (respiratory support)
- Basil (digestive and calming)
- Dill (gas-relieving and cooling)

1. Basil & Oregano Herbal Salt

Purpose: Antimicrobial seasoning for daily use
Ingredients:

- 3 tbsp dried basil
- 2 tbsp dried oregano
- ½ cup Himalayan or sea salt

Instructions:
Grind together to a fine powder. Store in spice jar.

Use: Sprinkle on veggies, meats, pasta, or pizza.
Caution: None for general use.

2. Rosemary & Sage Cooking Salt

Purpose: Enhances memory, supports digestion
Ingredients:

- 2 tbsp dried rosemary
- 2 tbsp dried sage
- ½ cup mineral salt

Instructions:
Pulse until powdery. Store sealed in a cool, dry place.

Use: Delicious in breads, roasted potatoes, and poultry.
Caution: Sage is strong—moderate if pregnant or nursing.

3. Holy Basil & Lemon Zest Salt

Purpose: Uplifting, calming adrenal support
Ingredients:

- 2 tbsp dried Holy Basil (Tulsi)
- 1 tsp lemon zest (dried)
- ½ cup salt

Instructions:
Blend and jar. Label with name and date.

Use: Sprinkle over avocado toast, rice, or steamed veggies.
Caution: May lower blood sugar—monitor if diabetic.

Herbal Butters

Herbal butters are creamy, nutrient-rich spreads that turn ordinary bread, pasta, or steamed veggies into gourmet herbal delights.
They're also a fun way to sneak healing herbs into children's meals or turn everyday cooking into medicine.

Great Combinations:

- **Lemon balm + honey** – calming, sweet, ideal on toast
- **Basil + garlic** – classic pesto-style flavor for pasta or bread

- **Lavender + maple syrup** – unique, floral-sweet spread for breakfast scones or muffins

Storage Tip:
Form into logs and freeze. Slice off coins as needed. Keeps 1–2 months in fridge, 3–6 months in freezer.

1. Lemon Balm & Honey Butter

Purpose: Nervine, mild anxiety and sleep support
Ingredients:

- 1 stick unsalted butter (softened)
- 1 tbsp finely chopped fresh lemon balm
- 1 tsp honey

Instructions:
Blend and refrigerate in parchment. Use within 5–7 days.

Use: Spread on toast before bed or over warm muffins.
Caution: Avoid with hypothyroid conditions unless approved.

2. Garlic & Basil Compound Butter

Purpose: Immune support, cardiovascular protection
Ingredients:

- ½ stick butter
- 1 tbsp minced garlic
- 1 tbsp fresh or dried basil
- Pinch sea salt

Instructions:
Combine all ingredients. Chill. Use within 1 week.

Use: Spread over pasta, warm bread, or grilled meats.
Caution: Garlic can irritate sensitive stomachs.

3. Lavender Maple Breakfast Butter

Purpose: Comforting, calming, gentle digestive aid
Ingredients:

- 1 stick butter
- 1 tsp dried lavender
- 1 tsp maple syrup

Instructions:
Soften butter, stir in ingredients, roll into log and refrigerate.

Use: Spread on pancakes, scones, or cornbread.
Caution: Start with small amount; lavender is strong in flavor.

4. Dill & Chive Potato Butter

Purpose: Supports digestion, adds fresh herbal flavor
Ingredients:

- 1 stick butter
- 1 tbsp chopped fresh dill
- 1 tbsp fresh chives

Instructions:
Blend well, refrigerate, use within 1 week.

Use: Melt over roasted potatoes or fish.
Caution: Use fresh herbs quickly; do not store if watery.

50 Herbal Recipes for Culinary Meals, Drinks & Treats

Hearty Meals, Soups, Bowls, and Nourishing Mains

1. Immune Boosting Nettle & Miso Soup

Purpose: Rebuilds minerals, supports immunity, gently detoxifies

Ingredients:

- 1 tbsp dried nettle
- 1 tsp dried thyme

- 1 tbsp dried shiitake mushrooms
- 1 tsp grated ginger
- 2 tbsp miso paste
- 4 cups vegetable broth

Instructions:

1. Simmer nettle, thyme, mushrooms, and ginger in broth for 20 minutes.
2. Turn off heat. Stir in miso gently (do not boil).
3. Strain if preferred or blend for smoother texture.

Use: Best taken during or after illness, or for mineral support.
Caution: Avoid nettle in cases of kidney disease unless supervised.

2. Red Clover Hormone Balance Stew

Purpose: Supports lymphatic cleansing and hormone regulation

Ingredients:

- 1 tbsp red clover blossoms
- 1 cup diced sweet potato
- ½ cup chopped beets
- 1 cup cooked lentils
- 1 tsp dried rosemary
- 4 cups broth

Instructions:

1. Simmer all ingredients together for 30–40 minutes.
2. Season to taste and serve warm.

Use: Ideal in the menstrual follicular phase or gentle spring detox.
Caution: Avoid in estrogen-sensitive conditions.

3. Holy Basil (Tulsi) Nourish Bowl

Purpose: Adaptogen for stress resilience and energy

Ingredients:

- 1 tbsp dried Tulsi

- 1 cup red lentils
- 1 tsp turmeric
- ½ tsp cumin
- 4 cups water or broth
- Salt to taste

Instructions:

1. Simmer lentils with Tulsi and spices until soft (20–25 min).
2. Serve over cooked rice or quinoa.

Use: Great for work recovery or fatigue.
Caution: May affect blood sugar. Monitor if diabetic.

4. Calendula Carrot Gut-Soothing Soup

Purpose: Supports digestive healing and reduces gut inflammation

Ingredients:

- 1 tbsp dried calendula petals
- 1 cup chopped carrots
- ½ onion
- 1 clove garlic
- 1 tbsp olive oil
- 4 cups veggie broth

Instructions:

1. Sauté onion and garlic in olive oil.
2. Add carrots, calendula, and broth. Simmer 20 min.
3. Blend smooth or serve chunky.

Use: After stomach upset, indigestion, or antibiotics.
Caution: Calendula is in the daisy family—avoid if allergic.

5. Rosemary Root Veggie Tray Bake

Purpose: Enhances circulation, memory, and grounding

Ingredients:

- 2 tsp dried rosemary
- 1 sweet potato (cubed)
- 2 carrots
- 1 beet
- 1 tbsp olive oil
- Salt to taste

Instructions:

1. Toss veggies with rosemary, oil, and salt.
2. Roast at 400°F for 40–45 minutes until golden.

Use: Serve warm with lentils or proteins.
Caution: Use rosemary sparingly in pregnancy.

6. Lavender & Chamomile Quinoa Porridge

Purpose: Nervous system support, restful sleep

Ingredients:

- 1 cup cooked quinoa
- 1 cup chamomile + lavender tea (steeped)
- 1 tbsp maple syrup
- 1 tsp coconut oil
- Pinch of cinnamon

Instructions:

1. Simmer quinoa with tea and coconut oil until thick.
2. Stir in maple syrup and cinnamon.

Use: Perfect for winding down or gentle mornings.
Caution: Lavender may be too aromatic for children—reduce amount.

7. Garlic, Basil & Chickpea Stir Fry

Purpose: Supports digestion, immune function, and energy

Ingredients:

- 1 cup cooked chickpeas

- 1 tbsp olive oil
- 2 cloves garlic
- 1 tsp dried basil
- 1 cup chopped kale

Instructions:

1. Sauté garlic and basil in olive oil.
2. Add chickpeas and kale, cook until tender.

Use: Quick and energizing lunch or dinner.
Caution: Avoid garlic if prone to reflux.

8. St. John's Wort Veggie Broth

Purpose: Mood support, nerve soothing

Ingredients:

- 1 tbsp St. John's Wort
- ½ cup chopped celery
- ½ cup chopped carrots
- ¼ chopped onion
- 4 cups broth

Instructions:

1. Simmer all ingredients for 30 min.
2. Strain and sip warm.

Use: For low mood or nervous tension.
Caution: May interact with medications. Avoid during pregnancy.

9. Thyme Lentil Chili

Purpose: Respiratory health, warmth, digestion

Ingredients:

- 1 cup lentils
- 1 tbsp thyme
- 1 tsp cumin

- 1 clove garlic
- ½ chopped tomato
- 4 cups water

Instructions:

1. Simmer all ingredients until lentils are tender (35–40 min).
2. Adjust spices and serve.

Use: Ideal in cold weather.
Caution: Thyme may stimulate menstruation—use moderately.

10. Lemon Balm Couscous Salad

Purpose: Nervine, calming, digestive

Ingredients:

- 1 cup cooked couscous
- 2 tbsp chopped lemon balm
- 1 tbsp lemon juice
- 1 tbsp olive oil
- Salt and pepper

Instructions:

1. Combine all ingredients.
2. Chill and serve as side or lunch.

Use: Uplifting meal prep for stress.
Caution: Monitor thyroid health when using lemon balm regularly.

11. Garlic & Nettle Pasta Toss

Purpose: Builds blood, aids detox, supports digestion

Ingredients:

- 1 cup cooked pasta (any variety)
- 1 cup steamed nettle leaves (or sautéed if fresh)
- 2 cloves garlic, minced
- 1 tbsp olive oil

- Salt and pepper to taste

Instructions:

1. Sauté garlic in olive oil until fragrant.
2. Add nettle leaves and stir until wilted (or use pre-steamed).
3. Toss with warm pasta. Season to taste.

Use: A mineral-rich weekday meal.
Caution: Nettle must be fully cooked; raw leaves sting.

12. Mint & Basil Watermelon Salad

Purpose: Cooling, uplifting, and digestive aid

Ingredients:

- 2 cups watermelon cubes
- 1 tbsp chopped fresh mint
- 1 tbsp chopped fresh basil
- Juice of ½ lime
- Pinch of sea salt

Instructions:

1. Combine all ingredients in a bowl.
2. Toss gently and chill before serving.

Use: Excellent as a summer hydration boost or party side.
Caution: None. Very gentle and kid-friendly.

13. Dandelion Green Frittata

Purpose: Liver-supportive, rich in minerals and bitter tonics

Ingredients:

- 1 cup dandelion greens (blanched or chopped)
- 4–6 eggs
- ¼ cup chopped onion
- 1 clove garlic, minced
- 2 tbsp olive oil

- Pinch of salt and pepper

Instructions:

1. Sauté onion and garlic in olive oil.
2. Add greens and cook down.
3. Whisk eggs, pour into pan, cook on stove or bake at 350°F until set.

Use: Breakfast or protein-rich lunch.
Caution: Dandelion is bitter—blend with spinach for mild taste.

14. Chamomile & Apple Oatmeal Bake

Purpose: Eases digestion, soothes anxiety, great for kids

Ingredients:

- 1 cup oats
- 1 cup chamomile tea (infused and cooled)
- 1 grated apple
- 1 tbsp maple syrup
- 1 tsp cinnamon
- 1 egg (or flax egg)

Instructions:

1. Combine all ingredients.
2. Pour into greased baking dish.
3. Bake at 350°F for 25–30 minutes.

Use: For school mornings or after-school snacks.
Caution: Check for daisy family allergies before giving to children.

15. Holy Basil Immune Mushroom Soup

Purpose: Deep adaptogenic immune support

Ingredients:

- 1 tbsp dried holy basil (Tulsi)
- 1 cup chopped mushrooms (shiitake or button)
- ½ onion, diced

- 2 cloves garlic
- 1 tsp tamari or soy sauce
- 4 cups vegetable broth

Instructions:

1. Sauté onion and garlic. Add mushrooms.
2. Pour in broth, Tulsi, and tamari.
3. Simmer for 25 minutes. Strain if desired.

Use: Best for fall or winter nourishment.
Caution: Tulsi may interact with blood thinners or diabetes meds.

16. Sage & White Bean Stew

Purpose: Supports digestion, enhances immunity, and provides warmth

Ingredients:

- 1 tbsp dried sage
- 2 cups vegetable broth
- 1 cup cooked white beans
- ½ cup chopped carrots
- 1 clove garlic, minced
- Salt and olive oil to finish

Instructions:

1. Simmer broth, sage, garlic, and carrots for 15 minutes.
2. Add beans and cook until warmed through.
3. Season with salt and a drizzle of olive oil.

Use: Enjoy as a warming lunch or protein-rich dinner.
Caution: Sage may suppress lactation—avoid in breastfeeding unless advised.

17. Fennel Lentil Sauté Bowl

Purpose: Aids digestion and reduces bloating

Ingredients:

- 1 tsp crushed fennel seeds

- 1 cup cooked lentils
- 1 cup chopped spinach
- 1 tbsp olive oil
- ½ tsp turmeric
- Salt and black pepper to taste

Instructions:

1. Sauté fennel and turmeric in oil.
2. Add spinach and stir until wilted.
3. Mix in lentils and cook 5–7 minutes.

Use: A grounding bowl for lunch or early dinner.
Caution: Fennel can mimic estrogen—monitor for hormone-sensitive conditions.

18. Dandelion Detox Soup

Purpose: Liver detox and gentle cleansing

Ingredients:

- 1 cup chopped dandelion greens
- 2 cups broth
- 1 chopped zucchini
- 1 clove garlic
- ½ onion, diced
- Lemon juice to finish

Instructions:

1. Sauté onion and garlic.
2. Add zucchini and broth, bring to simmer.
3. Add dandelion and cook 10 minutes.
4. Squeeze lemon over before serving.

Use: A spring cleanse or light detox dinner.
Caution: Dandelion is bitter—adjust to taste or mix with milder greens.

19. Lemon Balm Chickpea Pilaf

Purpose: Soothes nerves and supports digestion

Ingredients:

- 1 tbsp dried lemon balm
- 1 cup cooked chickpeas
- ½ cup cooked rice
- ¼ cup chopped cucumber
- 1 tbsp olive oil
- Salt to taste

Instructions:

1. Steep lemon balm in ½ cup hot water and cool.
2. Mix all ingredients in bowl.
3. Drizzle with infused water and oil. Chill and serve.

Use: A cooling lunch or summer prep dish.
Caution: Lemon balm may affect thyroid—use in moderation.

20. Thyme Sweet Potato Curry

Purpose: Warming, antimicrobial, and grounding

Ingredients:

- 1 tsp dried thyme
- 1 sweet potato, peeled and cubed
- ½ onion, chopped
- 1 clove garlic, minced
- ½ tsp curry powder
- 2 cups coconut milk or broth

Instructions:

1. Sauté onion, garlic, and curry powder.
2. Add sweet potato and liquid. Simmer 20 minutes.
3. Stir in thyme in the last 5 minutes.

Use: Nourishing, hearty dinner.
Caution: Thyme may stimulate menstruation—monitor in early pregnancy.

21. Calendula Carrot Millet Bowl

Purpose: Soothes digestion, enhances skin clarity

Ingredients:

- 1 tbsp dried calendula petals
- ½ cup cooked millet
- ½ cup shredded carrots
- 1 tsp olive oil
- Pinch of sea salt

Instructions:

1. Steep calendula in ½ cup hot water for 10 minutes, then strain.
2. Toss millet and carrots with infused water and olive oil.
3. Season and serve warm or chilled.

Use: Great for gut healing and skin support.
Caution: Avoid if allergic to ragweed/daisy family.

22. Basil Tomato Brown Rice Risotto

Purpose: Supports gut health and provides comfort

Ingredients:

- 1 tbsp dried basil
- ½ cup brown rice
- 1 cup chopped tomatoes
- 1 tbsp olive oil
- 2 cups vegetable broth

Instructions:

1. Cook rice in broth with tomatoes.
2. Add basil and olive oil midway.
3. Stir frequently until creamy.

Use: Comforting main or side dish.
Caution: Basil in excess may affect blood pressure—moderate intake.

23. Red Clover Sweet Potato Mash

Purpose: Lymphatic support and nourishment

Ingredients:

- 1 tbsp red clover blossoms
- 1 medium sweet potato
- 1 tbsp coconut oil
- Pinch of cinnamon
- Salt to taste

Instructions:

1. Boil and mash sweet potato.
2. Steep red clover in ¼ cup hot water and strain.
3. Mix mash with red clover infusion, oil, cinnamon, and salt.

Use: Pair with proteins or grains.
Caution: Avoid in estrogen-sensitive individuals.

24. Garlic Thyme Lentil Stew

Purpose: Immune strengthening and antimicrobial

Ingredients:

- 2 cloves garlic, minced
- 1 tsp dried thyme
- 1 cup lentils
- ½ chopped carrot
- 4 cups broth

Instructions:

1. Sauté garlic, add carrots and lentils.
2. Add broth and thyme. Simmer 30 minutes.
3. Season and serve hot.

Use: Immune fortification during illness.
Caution: Garlic may irritate sensitive stomachs.

25. Oregano Quinoa Stuffed Peppers

Purpose: Antibacterial and nutrient-rich meal

Ingredients:

- 2 bell peppers (halved and cleaned)
- 1 cup cooked quinoa
- 1 tsp dried oregano
- ¼ cup corn
- 2 tbsp chopped onion

Instructions:

1. Mix quinoa, veggies, and oregano.
2. Stuff peppers, bake at 375°F for 25 minutes.

Use: Meal-prep friendly main.
Caution: Oregano is strong—moderate for kids.

26. Mallow Root Vegetable Hash

Purpose: Moistening and soothing to GI tract

Ingredients:

- 1 tbsp dried mallow (or marshmallow) root
- 1 cup diced root veggies (carrot, parsnip, beet)
- 1 tbsp olive oil
- Pinch sea salt

Instructions:

1. Steep mallow in warm water and set aside.
2. Sauté veggies until golden, drizzle with mallow infusion.

Use: For dry constipation or irritated gut.
Caution: Use clean, well-sourced mallow only.

27. Holy Basil Lentil Biryani

Purpose: Adaptogenic, digestive-friendly one-pot meal

Ingredients:

- 1 tbsp dried Tulsi
- 1 cup cooked lentils
- ½ cup cooked basmati rice
- 1 tsp cumin seeds
- 1 tsp ghee or oil

Instructions:

1. Toast cumin in ghee, add lentils and rice.
2. Steep Tulsi in ½ cup water, strain into mix.
3. Simmer 10 min and serve.

Use: Stress support lunch.
Caution: Monitor blood sugar if diabetic.

28. Dill & Carrot Vegan Patties

Purpose: Digestive, mildly cooling and flavorful

Ingredients:

- 1 tsp dried dill
- ½ cup shredded carrots
- ¼ cup cooked quinoa
- 2 tbsp oat flour
- Pinch salt

Instructions:

1. Mix all ingredients.
2. Form into patties and pan-fry or bake.

Use: Serve with dips or in wraps.
Caution: None known; gentle formula.

29. Chamomile Wild Rice & Apple Pilaf

Purpose: Nervine, gut-soothing, kid-friendly

Ingredients:

- 1 cup wild rice (cooked)

- 1 apple, diced
- 1 tbsp dried chamomile
- 1 tbsp butter or oil
- Dash cinnamon

Instructions:

1. Steep chamomile and strain.
2. Mix rice, apple, butter, and infusion.
3. Warm gently and season.

Use: Light dinner or breakfast.
Caution: Chamomile may cause drowsiness—avoid before driving.

30. Rosemary Black Bean Chili

Purpose: Circulatory support and protein-rich main

Ingredients:

- 1 cup cooked black beans
- 1 tsp dried rosemary
- ½ cup chopped tomato
- ¼ cup onion
- 1 tsp smoked paprika

Instructions:

1. Sauté onion, add tomato, beans, and rosemary.
2. Simmer 15 minutes. Adjust seasoning.

Use: Spicy and warming meal.
Caution: Rosemary may be stimulating for sensitive systems.

Nourishing Drinks, Smoothies, Treats, and Immune Tonics

31. Holy Basil & Honey Nightcap Tea

Purpose: Supports stress recovery, nervous system replenishment

Ingredients:

- 1 tbsp dried Holy Basil (Tulsi)
- 1 cup hot water
- 1 tsp raw honey
- Pinch of cinnamon

Instructions:

1. Steep Tulsi in hot water for 10–15 minutes.
2. Strain and stir in honey and cinnamon.
3. Drink warm before bed.

Use: Relaxing evening tonic.
Caution: May lower blood sugar or interact with blood thinners.

32. Red Clover & Strawberry Smoothie

Purpose: Lymphatic support and skin-nourishing antioxidants

Ingredients:

- 1 tbsp red clover blossoms (steeped and cooled)
- 1 cup fresh or frozen strawberries
- ½ banana
- 1 cup coconut milk or almond milk
- 1 tsp flax seeds

Instructions:

1. Brew red clover tea and cool.
2. Blend all ingredients until smooth.
3. Drink immediately or chill.

Use: Mid-morning or afternoon refreshment.
Caution: Avoid in estrogen-sensitive conditions.

33. Chamomile Lemon Detox Water

Purpose: Soothes digestion and nerves, gently detoxes liver

Ingredients:

- 1 tbsp dried chamomile
- ½ lemon, sliced
- 1 qt filtered water
- Optional: mint sprig

Instructions:

1. Steep chamomile in 1 cup hot water, cool.
2. Add tea and lemon to remaining water.
3. Chill and sip throughout the day.

Use: Daily hydration and calm.
Caution: Avoid if allergic to daisy-family plants.

34. Dandelion Root Cocoa Latte

Purpose: Liver support with chocolate comfort

Ingredients:

- 1 tbsp roasted dandelion root
- 1 tsp raw cacao powder
- 1 cup oat milk
- 1 tsp honey or maple syrup
- Pinch cinnamon

Instructions:

1. Simmer dandelion root in oat milk for 10 min.
2. Add cacao and sweetener, whisk well.
3. Strain and serve warm.

Use: Morning or afternoon coffee alternative.
Caution: Avoid if allergic to ragweed family.

35. Lavender & Blueberry Chia Pudding

Purpose: Calming, antioxidant-rich snack

Ingredients:

- 1 tsp dried lavender

- 1 cup almond milk
- ½ cup blueberries
- 2 tbsp chia seeds
- 1 tsp vanilla extract

Instructions:

1. Infuse almond milk with lavender, then strain.
2. Blend with blueberries and vanilla.
3. Stir in chia seeds. Refrigerate overnight.

Use: Chill and serve as dessert or breakfast.
Caution: Lavender can be overpowering—use sparingly.

36. Nettle Mineral Smoothie

Purpose: Replenishes iron and minerals; great for fatigue

Ingredients:

- 1 tbsp dried nettle (steeped and cooled)
- 1 banana
- ½ avocado
- 1 cup oat milk
- 1 tsp spirulina or moringa (optional)

Instructions:

1. Blend all ingredients until creamy.
2. Drink immediately or chill.

Use: Energizing breakfast or post-workout boost.
Caution: May increase urination. Avoid with kidney issues.

37. Peppermint Cacao Energy Balls

Purpose: Refreshing focus, chocolate fix without crash

Ingredients:

- 1 cup dates (pitted)
- ¼ cup raw cacao

- 1 tbsp dried peppermint
- 1 tbsp almond butter
- ½ cup oats

Instructions:

1. Pulse everything in a food processor.
2. Roll into 1-inch balls.
3. Chill to firm.

Use: Afternoon pick-me-up.
Caution: Peppermint may aggravate reflux.

38. Ginger-Lemon Herbal Gelatin Cups

Purpose: Gut-healing, anti-inflammatory

Ingredients:

- 1 tbsp grated ginger
- Juice of 1 lemon
- 1 tbsp honey
- 1 cup water
- 1 tbsp grass-fed gelatin

Instructions:

1. Simmer ginger and lemon juice in water.
2. Stir in gelatin and honey. Pour into molds.
3. Chill until set.

Use: After meals or as healing snack.
Caution: Not suitable for vegans (use agar as alternative).

39. Cinnamon-Basil Apple Slices

Purpose: Balances blood sugar, calms cravings

Ingredients:

- 1 apple, sliced
- 1 tsp chopped fresh basil

- ¼ tsp cinnamon
- 1 tsp honey

Instructions:

1. Toss apple slices with basil, cinnamon, and honey.
2. Let sit 10 minutes before serving.

Use: Simple herbal snack.
Caution: Basil can lower blood pressure—monitor if on medication.

40. Fennel & Pear Digestive Compote

Purpose: Relieves bloating, aids digestion

Ingredients:

- 1 ripe pear, chopped
- ½ tsp fennel seeds
- ½ tsp ginger
- 1 tsp honey
- ¼ cup water

Instructions:

1. Simmer all ingredients until pear is soft.
2. Mash lightly and cool.

Use: As a dessert or after heavy meals.
Caution: Fennel may mimic estrogen—monitor if sensitive.

41. Tulsi-Cucumber Herbal Lemonade

Purpose: Cools body, reduces mental tension

Ingredients:

- 1 tbsp dried Tulsi
- 1 tbsp lemon juice
- 2 slices cucumber
- 1 tsp honey
- 1.5 cups water

Instructions:

1. Steep Tulsi tea and cool.
2. Blend with remaining ingredients and chill.

Use: Summer hydration tonic.
Caution: Use with caution if on blood thinners.

42. Rosemary & Orange Baked Sweet Potatoes

Purpose: Boosts circulation, antioxidant synergy

Ingredients:

- 2 medium sweet potatoes, sliced
- 1 tbsp olive oil
- 1 tsp dried rosemary
- Zest of ½ orange

Instructions:

1. Toss all ingredients together.
2. Bake at 375°F for 40 minutes.

Use: Side dish or nourishing dinner bowl base.
Caution: Rosemary can be drying in excess.

43. Hibiscus Lime Ice Pops

Purpose: Hydrating, cooling, high in vitamin C

Ingredients:

- 1 tbsp dried hibiscus
- Juice of 1 lime
- 1 tbsp honey
- 1.5 cups water

Instructions:

1. Steep hibiscus in water and cool.
2. Add lime and honey. Pour into molds.

3. Freeze overnight.

Use: Summer immune-boost.
Caution: May lower blood pressure.

44. Sage Infused Cornbread Muffins

Purpose: Antimicrobial and grounding with a savory twist

Ingredients:

- 1 cup cornmeal
- ½ cup flour
- 1 tsp baking powder
- 1 tbsp chopped sage
- 1 egg
- 1 cup milk
- 1 tbsp oil

Instructions:

1. Mix dry, then wet ingredients.
2. Fold in sage.
3. Bake at 375°F for 20 min.

Use: Pair with soups or stews.
Caution: Sage may suppress lactation in nursing women.

45. Herbal Chai with Cinnamon, Ginger & Holy Basil

Purpose: Warming, digestive, stress-relieving

Ingredients:

- 1 tsp dried holy basil
- ½ tsp cinnamon chips
- ½ tsp dried ginger
- 1 cup almond milk
- 1 tsp honey

Instructions:

1. Simmer herbs in almond milk for 10 minutes.
2. Strain and sweeten with honey.

Use: Midday recharge or digestive evening drink.
Caution: Ginger may interact with blood thinners.

46. Lemon Balm Cucumber Cooler

Purpose: Nervine, hydrating, and cooling for hot days

Ingredients:

- 1 tbsp dried lemon balm
- 2 slices fresh cucumber
- Juice of ½ lemon
- 1 tsp honey
- 1.5 cups cold water

Instructions:

1. Steep lemon balm in ½ cup hot water, let cool and strain.
2. Combine with cucumber, lemon juice, and honey.
3. Add cold water, stir, and serve over ice.

Use: Summer hydration and stress relief.
Caution: Lemon balm may interact with thyroid medications.

47. Mint & Tulsi Herbal Green Smoothie

Purpose: Refreshes mind, supports digestion and adrenal balance

Ingredients:

- 1 tbsp dried mint
- 1 tbsp dried tulsi
- ½ banana
- ½ cup spinach
- 1 cup almond milk or coconut water
- 1 tsp chia seeds

Instructions:

1. Brew a strong mint-tulsi infusion, let cool and strain.
2. Blend all ingredients until smooth.

Use: Post-workout recovery or cooling summer breakfast.
Caution: Tulsi may thin blood or lower blood sugar—monitor closely.

48. Ginger & Hibiscus Electrolyte Tonic

Purpose: Rehydrates and supports circulation

Ingredients:

- 1 tsp dried hibiscus
- ½ tsp grated fresh ginger
- 1.5 cups water
- 1 tsp honey
- Pinch of sea salt

Instructions:

1. Simmer hibiscus and ginger in water for 10 minutes.
2. Strain and stir in salt and honey. Cool before serving.

Use: Natural electrolyte drink after exertion.
Caution: Hibiscus may lower blood pressure—use cautiously.

49. Chamomile Golden Milk

Purpose: Calming, anti-inflammatory evening drink

Ingredients:

- 1 tbsp dried chamomile
- 1 cup warm almond or oat milk
- ½ tsp turmeric
- Pinch black pepper
- 1 tsp maple syrup

Instructions:

1. Steep chamomile in hot milk for 10–15 min.
2. Add turmeric, pepper, and sweetener. Strain and serve.

Use: Evening ritual to support sleep and gut health.
Caution: May cause drowsiness—avoid before activity requiring alertness.

50. Basil-Strawberry Immune Mocktail

Purpose: Immune and mood-lifting treat

Ingredients:

- 1 tbsp dried or 2 tbsp fresh basil
- ½ cup strawberry puree
- 1 tsp lime juice
- 1 tsp honey
- 1.5 cups sparkling water

Instructions:

1. Steep basil in ½ cup hot water and cool.
2. Mix with strawberry, lime, and honey.
3. Add sparkling water and serve chilled.

Use: Midday herbal celebration or gentle social drink.
Caution: Basil can affect blood clotting—monitor if on medication

Chapter 12

Living Seasonally

Living with the rhythms of the seasons is one of the most ancient and powerful ways to support wellness. Herbs respond to seasonal needs just as our bodies do—offering gentle cleanses in spring, cooling relief in summer, fortification in fall, and deep nourishment in winter.

This chapter outlines how to work with nature's cycles and tailor your herbal care for each season.

Spring: Cleansing & Liver Support

Spring marks the return of growth, movement, and light. It's a season of natural detoxification—both in nature and within the body. After winter's heaviness, the liver, lymphatic system, and digestion benefit from renewal and flow.

Key Herbs for Spring:

- **Dandelion root and leaf** – bitter, cleansing, liver-supportive
- **Nettle** – rich in minerals, toning, blood-strengthening
- **Red Clover** – lymphatic mover and gentle detoxifier
- **Burdock root** – purifying, cooling, and supportive to the skin

How to Use:

- Teas and infusions (daily, mild doses)
- Tinctures or vinegar extracts
- Add to spring broths, greens, and fresh juices

Tips:

Begin slowly and stay hydrated. Too much detox too fast may create fatigue or skin breakouts.

Summer: Cooling & Hydrating Herbs

Summer is bright, hot, and often depleting—especially to the nervous system, skin, and hydration levels. This is the time for herbs that **cool**, **relax**, and **restore** moisture to tissues.

Key Herbs for Summer:

- **Peppermint** – cooling, digestive, breath-freshening
- **Lemon Balm** – calming, mood-lifting, antiviral
- **Hibiscus** – tangy, rich in vitamin C, gently lowering blood pressure
- **Chamomile** – nervine, anti-inflammatory, skin-soothing

How to Use:

- Iced herbal teas and infusions
- Herbal lemonade with honey and citrus
- Freezer pops or herbal ice cubes

Tips:

Avoid diuretic or overly stimulating herbs in the heat. Choose gentle infusions and combine with fruits for hydration support.

Fall: Immune Fortification

Autumn brings transition—cooler air, increased dryness, and the beginning of cold/flu season. It's the season to **fortify** the immune system, **protect** the lungs, and nourish from within.

Key Herbs for Fall:

- **Echinacea** – immune stimulant (use short-term or preventatively)
- **Thyme** – respiratory disinfectant, antispasmodic
- **Astragalus root** – adaptogenic, deeply supportive to immunity
- **Elderberry** – antiviral, rich in antioxidants

How to Use:

- Syrups (especially elderberry)
- Decoctions with astragalus and warming herbs like ginger
- Herbal steams and broths

Tips:

Start using herbs early in the season—don't wait until illness hits. Combine with warming foods and routines that support the lungs.

Winter: Deep Nourishment & Restoration

Winter is nature's invitation to **rest, rebuild**, and **go inward**. The kidneys, nervous system, bones, and immune reservoirs are the focus. Choose deeply nourishing, mineral-rich herbs and warming preparations.

Key Herbs for Winter:

- **Oatstraw** – strengthens nerves, rich in silica and calcium
- **Marshmallow root** – soothing to mucous membranes
- **Cinnamon** – circulatory and digestive stimulant
- **Ginger** – warming, digestive, and immune-boosting
- **Ashwagandha** – adaptogen for fatigue, stress, and sleep

How to Use:

- Long infusions and milk-based elixirs
- Bone broths enriched with roots and barks
- Fire cider and warming teas

Tips:

Slow down and rest more. Use herbs consistently and gently to restore depleted systems.

Closing Thoughts

Well friend… you made it.

You've walked through roots and recipes, brewed teas and blended tinctures, peeked inside leaves and learned how to welcome plants into your life—not just as ingredients, but as companions.

And here's the truth: this isn't really the end. It's the beginning of something wonderfully green.

Because once you start to see plants not just as "things" in jars, but as living allies that have helped humans for thousands of years—something shifts. You notice more. You slow down. You trust your body. You walk outside and recognize the lemon balm by its scent, the chamomile by its gentle blooms, the nettle by its prickly persistence.

This book wasn't written to turn you into a master herbalist overnight (though you're doing amazing, by the way). It was written to remind you that you already *know* how to care for yourself—you just needed the plants to help you remember.

May this book be your companion as you grow your own apothecary—of jars, of memories, of trust. May you come to know not just *what* herbs do, but *who* they are. And may your own healing ripple outward—to family, community, and beyond.

So keep going.
Keep growing.
Keep steeping, tasting, planting, and playing.
Keep listening—to your body, your intuition, and the whispers in the garden.

And when in doubt?

Make a cup of tea. Sit under a tree. Breathe.
The plants got your back.

With joy, dirt under the nails, and a heart full of herbs,
— **Maeven**

www.ingramcontent.com/pod-product-compliance
Lightning Source LLC
Chambersburg PA
CBHW052112020426
42335CB00021B/2725